How to Master Forex Trading!

By Dr. Scott Brown

How to Master Forex Trading!

© 2010 Four Winds Trading, Inc. All Rights Reserved.

www.TheBestBusinessOnEarth.com

CONTENTS

ABOUT THE AUTHOR

Dr. Scott Brown's biography is classic *"Rags to Riches"* Horatio Alger going from living in his pickup truck (or on any sympathetic acquaintance's couch in the freezing winter) to entrepreneur to trader to real estate investor and finally to university investment professor. He holds a Ph.D. in finance from the University of South Carolina and an MBA from Thunderbird, The American Graduate School of International Management in Phoenix, Arizona, ranked #1 by the U.S. News and World Report. His doctoral dissertation in futures and Forex trading attracted the interest and sponsorship of the Chicago Board of Trade.

The author of numerous investment how-to-books, courses, and seminars, Dr. Brown is an outspoken advocate of self-employment, self-investment, and self-enrichment through introspection, study, and self motivated action.

Dr. Brown is a 31 year veteran of the equity, bonds, futures, Forex, and options markets. In addition to leading up the Trade Mentors trading club Dr. Brown is a tenured associate professor of finance at the University of Puerto Rico's Graduate School of Business where he teaches doctoral and MBA investments, corporate finance, asset pricing, financial theory, and derivative trading classes. He is also the author of the highly recognized Trade Mentors advanced Forex curriculum at http://www.tradementors.com/

FREEDOM IS NOWHERE!

On A Mission without Permission

There are millions of people who **BELIEVE** themselves *"doomed"* to poverty and failure, because of some strange force over which they **BELIEVE** they have no control.

They are the creators of their own *"misfortunes,"* because of this negative **BELIEF**, which is picked up by the unconscious mind, and translated into its physical equivalent.

This is an appropriate place at which to suggest again that you may benefit, by passing on to your unconscious mind, any **DESIRE** which you wish translated into the physical, or monetary equivalent, in a state of expectancy or **BELIEF** that the transmutation will actually take place.

(Napoleon Hill in Think and Grow Rich)

FREEDOM IS
NOW HERE!

INTRODUCTION

*"I first applied for a job at Merrill Lynch, the stockbrokers. They asked, "College degree?'
I said, 'No.' so they said, 'No job.' The next day I applied to Bache and when they asked,
'College degree?' I said 'Yes.' It was an instant degree."*

—Muriel Siebert

*"When you find many people applauding you for what you do, and a few condemning,
you can be certain that you are on the wrong course because you're doing things that
fools approve of."*

—E.W. Scripps

*"Let money work for you, and you have the most devoted servant in the world…. There
is nothing animate or inanimate that will work so faithfully as money … It works night
and day, and in wet or dry weather."*

—P.T. Barnum

How to Master Forex Trading is about freedom. It's directed to the crowning
accomplishment of your ambitions, goals, and dreams. And it's about **YOUR**
freedom. This course is unlike anything you've ever seen before. It's different than
anything you've ever studied. How to Master Forex Trading gives you a **clear
path**; the exact precise action steps that will give you freedom to live the life
you've always wanted to live.

It does this by bringing all your ambitions, goals, and dreams to life in your life.

Have you seen Publisher's Clearing House (PCH) randomly give away millions to
absolute strangers? The Prize Patrol Team representing PCH knocked on Pamela
Barton's door on live TV in 2009 and handed her a certified check tax-free for ten-
million dollars.

Suppose the **Prize Patrol Team** knocked on your door tonight and handed **you** ten million dollars. What would you do with all that money?

Make a list. Go get a big yellow notepad, napkin, or scrap of paper **RIGHT NOW**…you have my permission. Be specific and write everything down right now.

Would you run out and get new car? What make of car would it be (Mercedes, Ferrari, Bentley, etc.)? What would the interior look like? Would you go for the fine smell of rich leather? Or do you prefer cloth seats?

Most folks would buy a new house. Would you? What architecture (prairie, craftsman, or modern)? How many bedrooms would your new home have? Would you have as many bathrooms as bedrooms? Would you have a heated infinity pool with a built in Jacuzzi and outdoor bathroom so that party guests don't track water into the house? Where in the world would your dream house be located? Bali, Vail, Monte Carlo, Australia, or Big Sur!

Would you travel to all the places you've dreamed of experiencing? Where specifically would you go? India, China, Brazil, South Africa's Exclusive Luxury Blue Train? Don't forget: Money's no matter as you write your desires on your notepad! Is there a way you have always wanted to help the world you feel strongly about? Would you go on mission to help bring potable water to a Bolivian village?

You could furnish your home with the finest designs, or maybe buy a yacht. What make and model would the yacht be? What color would you have the yacht company detail it?

Is one of your strong desires you jotted down *"financial freedom"*? How would you keep from losing your fortune? Where are the safe investments that beat inflation so that you keep it and grow it?

What about stable relationships? J. Paul Getty was a keen businessman but an atrocious husband and father.   He tore through marriage after marriage; was unfaithful; and used his last will and testament as a blunt instrument of terror to keep his inheritors in line.

Not everything of value is financial!

Keep going. List everything you dream of. If you're building your dream list in the privacy of you're home nobody is looking over you shoulder. You can write anything you want without fear of criticism. Keep writing. Do this **NOW**!

When you finish look over this list of yours. Did you dream bigger when you were younger? Did you have higher aspirations when you were in high school, college, or in the military? Are you dreams more "*sensible*?"

Have you lost your courage to **believe in yourself**?

Most people get beaten down over time in a world where adults play king of the hill. Few folks make it out of a corporate cubicle to the board of directors. In fact, our schools teach that only a small percentage of people can be successful. Isn't that what the teacher says when s/he tells the class at the beginning that only 10% or so will get an A?

How about the college professor who teaches an impossible class as they state that they keep the A's for themselves! All this reinforces a commonly held thinking system based on scarcity and lack where only a small few are arbitrarily deemed "*worthy*" to have enough or more than enough.

Most people get trampled under in the mad dash climb to the top of the **American Corporate Ladder**. And as society beats, stomps, and whips it's so called idea of what meager share it thinks most folks deserve the sparkle goes out of their eyes little by little each year that passes.

And their dream list gets more and more meager; less and less courageous.

Folks who, a decade or so back, wanted to lounge on their yacht settle for a scale plastic model for their home office. It gathers dust over time till their spouse throws it in the trash. People who desired an Armani wardrobe try to find the closest imitation on JC Penney's bargain rack!

Remember the guy in high school who always drew Ferraris on his note pad in class? Now he drives a truck the company he works for owns. And he drives a 15 year old Subaru to get to his truck driving job. How about those high school do good-ers? How much did they give to help families crushed in the Haiti earthquake?

I'm sure you must have pondered over your dream home when you were younger. Did your dream of a dream home vaporize into an apartment you rent or a tract home you hide in?

As cartoonist Harold Gray advised, "*The world is for those who make their dreams come true.*" **Your** dreams can become your reality! 1970's evangelist Reverend Ike said, "*Inflation, Recession, Depression? You don't have to participate!*" Ike's right!

Believe me when I say you don't have to participate.

That shrinking dream list of yours can be revived and transmuted into a large dream income. Simple! ***Do you want to increase your income?*** This isn't obvious to the vast majority of people. You have to give this some sincere thought. What the mind conceives and believes it **CAN** achieve. But not by half conceiving or half believing.

Now I'm going to ask you the most serious question you've likely **never** seriously considered.

Do you want to increase your wealth, net worth, and income? Stop. Ponder before continuing. Consider this question very carefully.

■■■■ PONDER CAREFULLY BEFORE CONTINUING ■■■■

Write down your answer: _____.

There's a slight hiccup. This problem may seem small right now but as you progress through this course you'll see it really is minor once you rearrange your thinking. Walk out to the street in front of your home early tomorrow morning. You'll hear *"click, clack, or ding."* Or even, *"wake up!"* in all the homes or apartments around you.

Rise and shine calls echo all over your neighborhood bright and early. And right after all the wake up noise, you'll hear something else. It won't be exclamations of, *"Wow...I get to go to my job again today!"* As they jump into their economy cars and head out for a peculiar activity called a 9 to 5 *"J" "O" "B."* Or a struggling family company they have to tend to that's really a 7 to 10 *"J" "O" "B."*

Blurry eyed they go to their cubicle, service desk, or steering wheel Monday morning and drag back in Monday night. Then they go out again early Tuesday morning, and come back in again Tuesday night. They go to work on Wednesday, crawl back Wednesday night thinking at least that they are over the *"hump."* Thursday it's the same; Friday it's no different. Then they put in a little unpaid overtime on Saturday or Sunday as a *"favor"* (because their boss reminds them how lucky they are to have their *"J" "O" "B"* in the bad economy their overpaid [still] executives brought on). Take a really hard look at folks that have treaded this treadmill for twenty, thirty or forty years. Ask yourself what they have achieved?

The sparkle is gone from their eyes, the tires are old on their cars, their bodies are worn, and their spirits low.

This *"J" "O" "B"* owns nearly all of your time. It commands when you can rest and relax. And it orders when you can't. It even decides when you can or cannot go on vacation. Your *"J" "O" "B"* dictates nearly every part of your life and you can't imagine living without it.

And when you're sixty five, you'll want to retire but can't. The fat cat executives who never did the hard work will have walked away with your retirement pension through their big bonuses. Your **butt** was tired from sitting at a desk but now your feet will be tired from greeting shoppers at Super Duper Mart.

Government studies reveal that the average U.S. retirement savings is a meager twenty five thousand dollars; the average income is but $1,705 a month!

Now calculate how much it costs you to live right now to get by. Think how it would be to live on $1,705 a month. What would you cut out? Would you live on dog food like some elderly retirees do today? Remember that this $1,705 includes social security which may or may not be around when you retire. A 2005 study found 40% of America's sicker adults did not fill a prescription because of cost.

According to the U.S. Census Bureau half of all retirees today live on LESS than $1,705 a month.

I know a 65 year old woman in Orlando, Florida who's worked for Disney Corporation for 27 years. She was well paid as a chef in Disney World, she retired and now receives $895 a month! *"What do you have planned?,* I asked. *"I'm here to get ideas from you:"* she admitted, *"Otherwise I'd have to move into an elderly coop."*

Did you feel a tinge of sadness for her?

Don't feel sorry for this woman. She's taking the bull by the horns and wrestling it to the ground. By taking action thinking for herself she's put herself ahead of game. However, it is sad that even though retirement seems like it's a long way off for most of us, we keep procrastinating planning until the bear trap snaps our ankle.

Yet 97% of Americans live like this. Their feet hit the floor early every morning at exactly the same time every day. They dress, generally skip a nice, relaxed breakfast, start their (bank loan owned) cars, then risk life and limb in traffic to punch in on time. Unless they get cut off at an intersection, they're late and in hot water! Otherwise, they're ahead of schedule and wait unpaid minutes before their shift starts.

But most mornings they ignore the stress of getting to and through work; it's become a "*natural*" part of their life.

This is peachy for some folks; they live life this way just like Fred and Wilma do on the Flintstones. But I'm talking about YOU now. I don't know you on one hand but on the other I think I really do. I know you deeply desire something better. I'm here to tell you that there is something better — heaps better — I wrote this course to tell you this.

The masses are taught to comply. Like animals to a slaughter house they go from the feedlot (school) to the loading ramp ("*J*" "*O*" "*B*") and finally get to the slaughterman's bolt gun (inadequate retirement). Most people live like this but there's so much more available for those who decide to stop following their downtrodden fellow man.

Plato's Allegory of the Cave is about people who have been chained in darkness for so long that they think shadows are real. When one of them breaks free, sees the light, and returns to tell the truth the rest try to kill him! Just try to tell you friends and neighbors that the old formula of go to school, get an education (any will do), go out and get a "*J*" "*O*" "*B*", work real hard, and life will be hunky dory plan doesn't work anymore. That's what's been rammed down your throat all your

14

life? Right? The reality is that with the second American Depression, that started in 2007, not only are students struggling to pay their loans; the money they're spending to repay them is worth-less.

That's not a pun… I meant worth-less and worthless!

So today even your education can force you to bankruptcy! That's a harsh statement when you consider that I AM a university professor whose salary is paid through all those student loans.

This is called BRINGIN IN THE BACON. This course teaches you something altogether different. How to Master Forex Trading is all about MAKING BACON! Which is more fun? BRINGIN IN THE BACON or MAKING BACON?

Ever get annoyed at the veneer of bliss of your coworkers who've recently attended self help seminars? They grow angry when you ask, "*Well if this get rich quick wealthy mind seminar is so great, why isn't everybody doing it instantly rich?!*" The reason is that these seminars give a lot of catchy sounding phrases but don't back it all up with specific steps. You know this because you've grown frustrated with thousand dollar (or more) bootcamps driven by clever marketing instead of true grit real workable wealth creating action steps!

The reality is that wealth is all around you but you need the specific code to crack the vault wide open. That's what this course is all about.

And $1,705 a month is forced poverty, so I am not stretching things when I say that most Americans are fading away — dying of thirst in the middle of a fresh water lake they can't see.

So when you're assessing some self help program, REMEMBER THAT THE MAJORITY ARE CREATED TO LINE THE POCKETS OF CLEVER MARKETERS. If you want real change in your life you have to come up with your own plan based on what works. You have to follow that plan diligently in the days, weeks, months, and years to come.

Less than 5% of the people in the world are following the beat of their own drum. If you look to others for advice and reassurance there's a 95% chance that the feedback, thoughts, reactions, warnings, and opinions will be flat out wrong or even detrimental to your success.

The people you've been looking to for guidance in mapping out your path in life are undoubtedly interested in your welfare but they are operating from a commonly held yet dysfunctional thought system. Because this faulty thought system is so widely held 95% of those you could look to for guidance are WRONG.

It's a struggle to smile, nod, yet ignore them; they're often the folks closest to you — relatives, close family, friends, coworkers, your supervisor. Can you win against this back pressure? We all have a desire to belong in our families, peer groups, workplace, and community. You don't want to be banished, threatened with solitude, disliked, and considered strange or stupid. But to make a firm change in your life for the better you have to resist the **desire to belong**.

I was raised in a small farming community. And I farmed most of my youth. One day I announced that I was going to make a living selling my ideas and teaching people how to live better lives. I remember a number of the land-rich farmers growing physical commodities who asked, *"Who would pay for an idea?"* If I would have listened to them I wouldn't the success I am today as a finance professor, researcher, book and bestselling course author.

And then there's that **mean voice** in your head. You know which one I'm talking about. It says, *"If only I had done this instead of that,"* and *"If only I knew then what I know now,"* are some of its favorite numbers. You may think that's your voice in your head but its not and you have to STOP listening to it. You have to STOP making the past real to yourself.

And if you STOP and think about it, how do you REALLY know IF your past is real anyway! What if you made it all up from some arbitrary perspective based on your unspoken **belief** in some strange force that you think dooms you to poverty and failure.

Here's a secret.

Do you know what the biggest fear of that mean voice in your head is? It's terrified you might one day, maybe today, wake up and realize you've been making your life up all along. That mean voice is terrified that you finally recognize you're **not a victim of circumstance** and can decide NOT to LISTEN.

In terms of your fears, what if you recognized you made it all up?!

What if?! What if you took full responsibility for your THOUGHTS and ACTIONS?! Success might just naturally follow!

My mastermind friend, Daniel Hall, is a trial attorney who just finished a book on how people can get a fresh start erasing their criminal record. This is not a dubious endeavor.

The book is personally endorsed by Harvard Law professor Alan Dershowitz!

Daniel just interviewed Dave of **Dave's Killer Bread** for his Amazon.com book "*The Ultimate Guide to Second Chances: Legal Ways to Erase or Hide Your Criminal Background*." Dave stopped listening to that voice and went from a hardened criminal in and out of prison for 15 years, to culinary sensation.

Watch Dave's inspirational video at http://www.daveskillerbread.com/story.shtml where Dave say's, "*I just started seeing myself as being able to do whatever I wanted to do!*"

Dave finally realized that if he wanted to achieve his dreams, goals, and ambitions he would have to STOP listening to his wrong mind and START silently believing in his **unconscious right (correct) mind**. He finally realized that would have, could have, and should have wrong (incorrect) minded thinking not only leads nowhere but that…

HIS PAST DID NOT HAVE TO EQUAL HIS FUTURE!

The mean voice in your head DOESN'T want you to wake up to a better life but if you can do this the past will no longer equal the future for you. It's not easy, but if you're to get where you want, you'll have to do it with independent thinking…THERE'S NO OTHER WAY. "*My Way*" must become your new theme song!

Read carefully this part of Frank Sinatra's lyrics …

"Regrets, I've had a few
But then again, too few to mention
I did what I had to do and saw it through without exemption
I planned each charted course, each careful step along the byway
*And more, much more than this, I did it **my way**"*

As you succeed, those doubting Thomas's will eventually follow your lead, but you've got to blaze the path first, take the first step nobody else can take for you, same as nobody can think for you. It's rough, yet it's a small price to pay for prosperity that has always awaited you. It's always been there, waiting in its white, shining, pure brilliance!

I started this course alluding to the fact that many people believe that there is an unseen force holding them back. In fact, some believe in a wrathful creator seeking vengeance for past sins. Yet the same book these people follow says that our creator is love and only love.

How can a purely loving creator want anything but good for you?

The conclusion I have arrived at through study, introspection, and action is that the only force holding people back from fully enjoying life is their own stinking thinking. When you erase a computer virus from your computer you are essentially reprogramming it positively. Right now, today, you must make a decision to positively reclaim your mind by erasing your stinking thinking. Is this simple? Yes! Is this easy? No. But where will you be five, ten, fifteen, or twenty years from now if you don't start today?!

"Now you must learn that only infinite patience produces immediate effects."
— A Course in Miracles

Believe it or not you've already accomplished the miraculous. There are approximately 639 skeletal muscles in the human body. When you learned to walk you had to USE YOUR MIND to coordinate all of them together in a monumental feat of effort you scarcely remember today. Ditto on when you learned to speak. And this was easy street compared to other feats you've undoubtedly accomplished including surviving high school (I barely did), succeeding at a *"J" "O" "B"*, or maybe even wooing over your significant other! Holy cow what a wild road you've surely traveled.

If I'd have laid odds in Las Vegas on your success I would have set them at a billion to one that you'd have failed…yet here you are reading this course I've prepared literally just for you!

It's OK to become successful no matter what you think you've done in your past that you or others think you should be or have been punished for. Dave and his killer bread have shown us that. But moving forward can't happen in a willy-nilly fashion. I had you write down your goals, ambitions, and dreams at the beginning of this course for a reason.

Your new life will only come about if you have a clear plan and that starts with a list of what you want out of life. Have you ever been frustrated with a boss who can't seem to tell you exactly what s/he wants from you? Nobody can work for that kind of a boss. Your unconscious mind is your most powerful *"employee."* It has to do what you ask of it. But you have to command it with clarity.

You must ensure that all of the things on your list harm nobody. This is a very important step. If you can find anything on your list that gives reason it might hurt someone then you have to drop it. Carefully analyze and clean every part of your list to make sure that what you want is good for all. If you're married do this with your wife or husband until you both agree it's exactly what you want and hurts nobody — just the way you both want it.

Let me make it clear that becoming wealthy is a definite desire that to be materialized harms nobody if done through right minded thinking the way Dave has.

Your Dream List must evoke intensely strong, warmly positive, emotions from you. This generates the essential BURNING DESIRE Napoleon Hill describes as the *"Secret"* in his book, **THINK AND GROW RICH**.

If it takes a week or three (or longer) to perfect your Dream List, take the time to get this step of the **How to Master Forex Trading Program** right; otherwise you'll feel like you're trying to climb a sand dune with bare feet.

NEITHER SKIP THIS STEP NOR TAKE IT LIGHTLY!

This is a strangely powerful secret I learned from Tony Robbins that worked like a charm for me when I was building my dream list and living on people's couches as a down-and-out broke twenty something. Once you have your perfect Dream list find some place secret and hide it. As you hide it see yourself handing the list over to your higher self (your unconscious mind). Then **stop thinking** about your list. I personally don't understand why this works but I did it and I have achieved 99% of **everything** on my list from nearly three decades ago.

Napoleon Hill calls this last step of allowing the unconscious mind to manifest your dream list **TRANSMUTATION**!

The World's Richest Oilman's Rules for Success

J. Paul Getty emphasized that, *"To succeed in business, to reach the top, an individual must know all it is possible to know about that business,"* and that *"The individual who wants to reach the top in business must appreciate the might of the **force of habit** and must understand that practices are what create habits. He must be quick to break those habits that can break him and hasten to adopt those practices that will become the habits that help him achieve the success he desires."*

A good habit is to help others get what they want before you get what you want. Now this doesn't mean that you have to help everybody or even that everybody has to like you. A successful insurance salesperson is effective at helping people gain peace of mind at the best cost — to know that their loved ones are protected financially for in any tragedy.

In return the salesman receives a commission.

My brother was the president of a large agricultural corporation. His business expertise and calculated risks provided thousands of families worldwide with a basic necessity: food. He had to do massive volume, because the profit margin in the food business, from very high overhead, is very, very low — about 3%. He employed hundreds of people and helped other folks get what they wanted in addition to food: money through employment. The business flourished through his wise management and became a very large corporation (serving 15 international markets worldwide). He reaped large returns in all areas of his life.

On the other hand, he told me about another food company in California that, at first glance should be out of business. Yet it sets new record sales and profits each year growing and thriving consistently over time.

This company overprices its products (because its overhead costs are well above average in its industry. The business **never advertises** in a tactic its competitors initially considered outlandish. The enterprise also maintains an alarmingly high payroll by hiring more employees per square foot of retail space than its competitors need to operate efficiently!

How does this business beat all odds thriving year in and year out? It does so by not being the "*usual*" mass market provider of foods. It offers up highly specialized gourmet and certified organic fare. This particular food retailer only locates its stores in wealthy neighborhoods where the customers seek pampering as they willingly pay a little more for easy access to the highest quality foodstuffs available in the world today.

Advertising is not required in this market niche of wealthy discerning clientele. These high class homemakers know where these stores are and they aren't "*Wal-Mart shoppers.*" They willingly pay more not to have to wait in line to check out for their groceries. These stores have a higher payroll because they ensure that there are always enough checkers as well as sufficient drivers for direct delivery online ordering to ensure no lines!

A small army of merchandisers do nothing but walk around all day long organizing and cleaning (instead of at night as in a normal supermarket). I tested this out. One day I dropped a scrap of waste and waited. Twenty seven seconds later it had disappeared into a dust pan! Have you ever realized that you forgot an item right when you're about to pay after a long wait in line? "*Oh the heck with it,*" you think,

"All those folks behind me will be angry," or *"I'll have to wait in line again. I'll just get it next time."* **No problem** in these stores! Just tell the clerk what you want and the item will immediately be brought up to you by a special radio headset linked employee just for that reason!

You won't have to pull your bags off the Rota Bagger like you would in Wal-Mart where the clerk pushes you out the cue as fast as possible. Your purchase will be neatly packed and a bagger will walk them to your car for you. You won't have to tip him because that's included in the higher prices for your groceries.

Another time, I entered the check-stand behind a woman who had just filled a second cart with Presto logs. Somebody commented and she said, *"My husband and I have a fireplace in our bedroom and we just love to wake up to a roaring fire on winter mornings for ambience."* I think this is fantastic. Wouldn't you love to wake up that way? What a positive way to start any day! Well what's wrong? Why don't you have a fireplace in your bedroom, if that's on your **DREAM LIST**?

Here's why — and this is my main reason behind writing The One Perfect Business: If you've attained peace of mind and material success enough for your needs and desires, your habits have been properly developed for success. If you have not attained your desires you have **NOT** developed and followed proper habits for success. The ability to form **HABITS** of our choosing is the one skill we are all blessed with in equal proportion. Our habits carry us to the White House or the poor house depending on which we choose.

What each of us does with this premeasured gift decides what we will experience in our lives.

If you don't like the way things are going in your life **NOW**, it's simply a matter of changing your habits! This part of the course is entitled *"On A Mission Without Permission!"* because **How to Master Forex Trading** can show you the way to your desires… all you have to do is to stop waiting for permission (that will never come) from family, friends and society to go it your way (not theirs) to your **DESIRES**, and **END** your, up-till-now, **POOR** use of time.

CHAPTER ONE: It's Zilch Till Somebody Buys

A marketing professor explained something to me one day that profoundly changed my thinking. No matter whom you are and what you do, **you're in business.**

Everybody is.

If you're an employee, you're selling your time and energy to your boss. If you're a cellular phone salesman, you earn income filling others' communication needs. Everybody's hawking something.

You're in business whether you like your livelihood or not.

But here's a secret few people understand. If you find something you really enjoy doing that fills a need, which you are also very good at or can become good at, doing work will never feel like work for you again. Let's say you hate your job now but find something else you like and can become GOOD at it… let's say you have a hobby of making great beer in your basement and after reading this course you poke around to find that there's a need in your community for a micro-brewery bar.

You may have been getting the signal to do so for years but haven't listened. What if, for instance, your friends and relatives have been enjoying your beer so much that they often comment that you should go into the beer business.

Of course, if they'd been thinking the way less than 5% of the population does they would have opened the bar themselves and hired you to brew the beer!

Many businesses start this way. You finally crank up the courage to agree to open your own brewery. You know beer brewing inside and out — you've got expertise and you convince all your relatives, neighbors, friends, and even the Small Business Administration to back the new business with loans.

What now?

You discover that the power bill is more than you thought. Advertising costs way more than the customers it brings in. The cost of barley tripled, and the cost of yeast and hops to make the beer quadrupled.

So one morning you awake out of business… in bankruptcy! You and your spouse simply lacked the cash (capital) to make it work — to your remorse.

On the other hand I have a friend named Brandon with a brewery as part of the bar. He makes horrible beer. His beer is so bad his friends don't drink in the bar even when he's there to throw his own birthday party…they bring their own. But Brandon's got money — lots and lots of money.

Brandon's got so much money when he makes a deposit his bank sends a limo!

Well Brandon heard that the micro-brewery business was a good one. So he decides to open his own place. Soon the word gets around, "*don't drink Brandon's crummy beer, it's the nastiest!*" And pretty soon Brandon's business is closed because he can't brew respectable beer.

This is what happens in the opposite situation of having lots of capital but no skill!

I'm not giving you extreme instances! The nightly news is loaded with misery of this sort. Recent Small Business Administration statistics show that 56% of new businesses fail in the first 4 years.

What's so fantastic about How to Master Forex Trading is that you can own your business for just $1,000 and not a penny more. So capitalization is a snap.

Another exciting part of the How to Master Forex Trading manual you're reading now is that it comes with all the basics needed to run your business(es).

They say it takes money to make money. That is true.

Working for the man in a job isn't going to get you anywhere in today's corrupted corporate America. In the past we fought the tyranny of the British crown. Now our CEOs have taken King George's place with an endless supply of dead-end corporate cubicles you don't have a breath of a chance of rising out of. I know — How to Master Forex Trading helped my wife escape from one.

So most people wisely decide to start their own business. And whether you have to protect the capital you've built up already or are mainly interested in accumulating enough capital to retire you're forced into a business that's yours. But what people who realize this don't do is look for businesses with the potential to make a lot of money from little capital. Here's why….

Let's carefully consider your *"opportunities"* from Investor's Business Daily's Investors.com website.

1. A Savings Deposit Account. A century ago you could just buy bonds, but not today – inflation withers these fixed income investments. Plus with today's interest rates at near zero; and with all the recent bank bail-outs and economy melt-downs it'll never happen again when these are good or safe investments. There is only one stark for sure economic truth that we've learned at the beginning of this century; we can't trust executives, banks, or the Federal government. I call this the "*new tyranny*" against American freedom.

2. A Stock Investing Account. I'm sure you're a bit aware of common stock because insiders switched out your pension for a 401(k). The stock market can definitely help you protect and gradually grow your capital, but it's not likely if you're starting out with nothing and working at a dead end, low pay job. This economy is not that of your father. Top corporate executives have interlocked all of the boards, control all of the media, own congress and won't let anybody but their cronies rise to the top. Without an analysis edge in education in stock analysis you'll be the last to know which of the fewer than 100 worthwhile stocks among over 15,000 in circulation will make it. And with all the overtime and extra jobs required for working America to stay afloat financially who has the time!

3. Life Insurance / Retirement Funds. The only way your family will profit from an insurance company is if you bite the dust well insured! And that's only if you knew enough about insurance not to get ripped off by the salesman. And starting with the pilots of US Airways the corporate insiders now have full license to steal your pension and never pay it back. So much for pensions… and do you know how terrified pensioners are that their fund will go belly up or that Social Security will change the rules?! Two to four hard working decades, then back to work as a Wal-Mart greeter when the money streams dries up.

So much for the American Dream of corporate "security!"

4. Bank Certificate of Deposit (CD). Look at item 1 again.

5. Other U.S. Federal Securities. Look at item 1 again.

6. Money Market CDs. Look at item 1 again.

7. Corporate Bonds / Commercial Paper. You're probably in the bond market because of your "*de-worsified*" mutual fund your employee recommended you buy in your 401(K) plan. Yet you probably know little else about them. And it sure sounds smart at a social gathering when a well-dressed couple says, "*we're diversified in stocks and bonds.*" Bonds are little different than earning interest on a savings account but inferior! When you buy a bond you're lending to corporate executives, or city, federal, and state bureaucrats for a certain amount of time in return for a fixed interest payment. If the bond comes due and the debt payers have survived, your original investment comes back.

Unlike FDIC secured savings accounts, bonds aren't guaranteed. Yet just like savings accounts inflation eats up your bond yield. Suppose you bought a $1,000 bond that pays 4.5% over a twenty year period today. Your broker's praises you on the good deal since rates are so low now. Inflation is 2.6%.

So your "*real*" yield is only 1.9%!

That's certainly not enough to retire on and not a good deal in my book. The bottom line in any fixed income investment (even high yield ones) is that you have to have a massive nest egg to begin with; you can't generate wealth this way with less than $2,500,000 as I teach my MBA students at the University of Puerto Rico.

8. Real Estate "Investments." Don't get me going on what an "*opportunity*" real estate is! People have made their fortunes in real estate. But invariably they had some other non-real estate cash cow business that paid off the mortgage. The reality is that real estate is no longer as easy as falling off a log, like it used to be. Government protects tenants. Tenants damage your properties in ways that should send them to prison. But again that's because they know that government protects tenants. And your misery in real estate doesn't stop there. Banks damaged the market with sub-prime lending. Then the banks got bailed out by government. Now these "*executive bonus*" banks refuse to lend you to repair tenant damage because the government didn't require them to loan back to taxpayers to help us better our lives! So you can't sell your houses and you're right back to tenants who are protected by the government. But you're not protected by anybody since you're not a social parasite or a fat cat CEO. So real estate has become the worst of all investments. The truth is that real estate is simply a distasteful business.

----- So we've considered your realistic possibilities for securing a wealthy future for your family and have come to the possibility of OWNING YOUR OWN BUSINESS. What do you think it takes to operate your own business?

Will you establish your business as a C-corp, S-corp, limited liability partnership, or sole proprietorship and do you understand the implications of each? **Who** will handle the legal issues and clarify your doubts about laws in your industry? Business experts are expensive. Accountants aren't cheap either. You'll have to start cheap with a solid bookkeeper who won't rob you blind (I know friends who've been through this).

Collection services work only if your clients can pay even otherwise it's like getting blood out of a stone for the average small business owner.

Will you need to carry inventory or maybe even hire a freight controller? How will you **pay** for inventory when your clients are short and need a little more time to pay? A bank loan just to cover payroll or to buy new inventory if a big client is slow to pay? How large is your promotion budget and are you sure it will bring in enough sales? Will you need the services of an agency or publicist and will they be effective?

If customers keep coming back for more will you be able to keep up your initial quality and supply continuity of your products? What staffing requirements will you have to have? Do you understand what you have to pay, when you have to **pay**, and what forms you have to provide? There's the **Occupational Safety and Health Administration (OSHA)**, workman's comp, and the Social Security System, Federal agencies, State Bureaucrats, and county *"form stampers"* to deal with (especially in a state like California where my brother lives).

What about retirement programs? Unions? Health Insurance? How easy is it for somebody to sue your business? Will you have enough capital to pull through economic downturns? Are you prepared emotionally, tactically, and strategically to run your business?

At least a few years, till it builds steam of its own?

If you're working now can you afford to let it go? What about basic overhead; mortgage or rent, utilities, janitorial services? What will become of your business? Got 4X the capital you think you need for the unexpected? Hell's Kitchen chef Gordon Ramsey has seen many new restaurants go bankrupt from bad publicity. How about odds for negative publicity?

Will your business go up then down on whims, fads, public opinion, strikes, boycotts, or natural disaster? Thought about competition? Will a new Wal-Mart in or near town destroy your business?

Do you understand how to comply with state and federal regulations that can damage or destroy your business. My brother tells me that he has to adhere to 243 pages of government regulations on diesel alone he sells in his gas station mini mart. Someone you pay, or you, yourself will have to constantly manage the operation — that means no days away for the first few years at least! How will you handle the unsettling danger of internal and external theft that could cost you your home, your marriage, and even your friendships?

If you've ever desired working on your own the way 99% of people envision owning a business, this summary of concerns has probably squashed your dream! Ask my friend and mastermind team member Lan Turner and he'll give you even more concerns since he manages 17 employees every day. When I walk through a fashion mall with my wife, I am amazed that ANY of the shops, stores, and restaurants is in business.

Hardly astonishing that 54% fail in the first 4 years !

Enough of the Bad and Ugly, Here's the Good

There's one perfect business that has none of these headaches.

The One Perfect Business:

- Will be managed alone by you.

- Has NO competition.

- Needs Neither record keepers nor auditors.

- Has NEITHER slow pay NOR uncollectible clients.

- Will NEVER lose more than you put into it (**REALLY IMPORTANT**).

- NEVER gets negative press.

- Is UNTOUCHED by fads, politics, or war.

- Needs NO inventory.

- Requires NO promotion.

- Doesn't Needs insurance.

- Doesn't require employees; hence neither workman's comp, employee benefits, payroll, nor payroll taxes will ever have to be paid by you out of your sales revenue.

- Has no exposure to either internal or external theft!

- Does not have sales or a need to build a customer list.

- Can be started with just $1,000 (strongly recommended) but NEVER more than $5,000.

- Is just as potentially profitable in a depression, stagflation, hyper-inflation, recession or war.

- Takes LITTLE time; men made wealthy by this business put in about 20 minutes a day and rarely more than 4.

- Lets you retire, semi-retire, vacation, or stay in your day job as you so DESIRE.

- Needs NO commercial office lease or physical facilities other than a kitchen table, computer, internet connection, $1,000, and some simple software costing less than that.

32

- Requires NEITHER an advanced education, university classes, nor special credentials; all the knowledge and know how you need to get started is in this course you're reading now.

- Is the only truly open ended business opportunity facing you now.

- Is powered by the EXACT same principle and force behind Microsoft, Google, Burger King, and every fortune-making business in the American free enterprise system: COMPOUNDING.

CHAPTER TWO: Einstein's Most Powerful Force!

Einstein was once asked what he considered to be the most powerful force in the universe. He replied, "*compound interest.*" Compounding is the essential factor in any successful, profit making endeavor, period. The classic example of the POWER and PRINCIPLE of COMPOUNDING is the story of the kid who asks his dad to make his allowance "*pennies-per-day.*" "*How do you want it?*" his father frowns. "*Shucks…,*" says the boy. "*It's the first day of March so just give me one cent now, two in the morning, four the next day, and so on. Then we'll start over at a penny each first day of the month.*"

This sounded like a deal to the father who was too busy to think it through since at first blush he thought he might save some money over his son's old allowance plan:

1-Mar	$ 0.01	17-Mar	$ 655.36
2-Mar	$ 0.02	18-Mar	$ 1,310.72
3-Mar	$ 0.04	19-Mar	$ 2,621.44
4-Mar	$ 0.08	20-Mar	$ 5,242.88
5-Mar	$ 0.16	21-Mar	$ 10,485.76
6-Mar	$ 0.32	22-Mar	$ 20,971.52
7-Mar	$ 0.64	23-Mar	$ 41,943.04
8-Mar	$ 1.28	24-Mar	$ 83,886.08
9-Mar	$ 2.56	25-Mar	$ 167,772.16
10-Mar	$ 5.12	26-Mar	$ 335,544.32
11-Mar	$ 10.24	27-Mar	$ 671,088.64
12-Mar	$ 20.48	28-Mar	$ 1,342,177.28
13-Mar	$ 40.96	29-Mar	$ 2,684,354.56
14-Mar	$ 81.92	30-Mar	$ 5,368,709.12
15-Mar	$ 163.84	31-Mar	**$ 10,737,418.24**
16-Mar	$ 327.68		

By day 5 dad figured out what was going on and shut the plan down — he realized his son would have earned over ten million on the last day of the month. Over the entire month he would have earned $21,474,836.47! Dad gingerly entered into gentlemanly agreements with his son after that!

A mere penny grows into millions effortlessly through the power of compounding. Multi-billionaire co-founder Larry Page got that way earning less than pennies on every one of the endless Google AdWords payments his company receives… Never underestimate the power of a penny expanding through compounding!

This is how the principle behind **How to Master Forex Trading** allowed currency trader **Michael Marcus** to go from near broke to $80 million rich with a house in every nice place in the world; some he almost never sleeps in. And he did it in a few short years!

Think of Dave when he first made that decision while sitting in a jail cell to transmute his dreams, goals, and ambitions into reality. What if you made killer bread like Dave? Say everybody raves about your bread and said you should go into business to sell it to the public.

You read the NOTHING HAPPENS UNTIL SOMEBODY BUYS chapter of this course, though you don't have the capital or the management expertise — and you don't want all those hassles and headaches! So you talk to two of your enthusiastic, bread loving friends and tell them you're selling bread out of your kitchen. You'll let them sell retail at $1.50 a loaf and they can buy from you wholesale at $0.75 per loaf.

Your neighborhood discovers that here's a way make money simply giving people what they want. Suddenly you neighbors willingly sell your bread for you. Your levering your time and hard work.

		YOU		

Sharon	Tom	Mildred	Jenny	Sarah

Revenue skyrockets, you're making more bread, and eager neighbors Sharon, Tom, Mildred, Jenny, and Sarah are paying bills and having a blast. You could go on this way, but over time you realize that **training** each neighbor to sell bread for you is time consuming — less efficient than putting your expertise into making more bread.

You're in the shower one day or eating a sandwich when suddenly an answer pops into your mind (isn't that funny about those perfect answers you get from time to time?): You teach Jenny and Tom to train others for you and give them a royalty override. They make more money themselves by multiplying their own efforts. Your bread revenue increases even more, and their recruits make extra money.

Everybody's happy, but what really just happened dawns on you. You're elated: now you're compounded!

Let's imagine this:

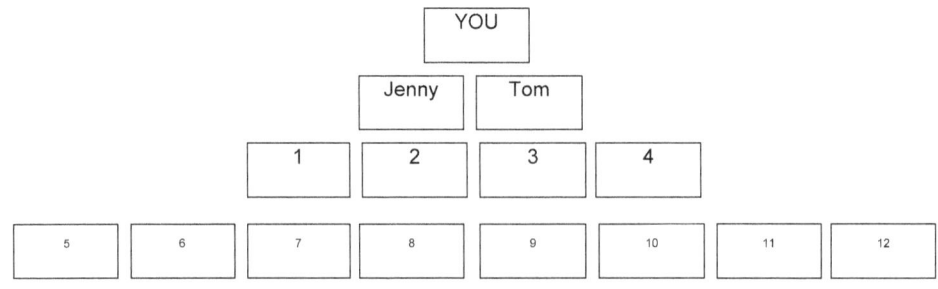

You taught **just 2 people** to sell bread, but now you have 12 bread-sellers buying from you!

If **you** had taught 12 bread-sellers personally, you wouldn't have enough hours in the day to train and bake bread for them to sell! Sure, at that point, you could employ a baker and bakery and train people all day long, or visa versa, but that would be building a CHAIN, not a PYRAMID. Chains are only as strong as their weakest link but pyramids are **strongest**.

Let's review:

You train 3 sellers:	3		(add 4!) 7
They " " " "	X 3		X 7
They " " " "	= 6		49
	X 3		X 7
They " " " "	=12		345
	X 3		X 7
	= 36	<--- Contrast! --->	= 2,401

That's real COMPOUNDING! This message is what all the referral marketing companies (Amway Global a.k.a. Quixar, Avon, Mary Kay, etcetera) are trying to teach their recruits. Those sellers who are successful at building networks get rich quick, but the vast majority of their down-lines don't understand or convey the simple lesson I've shared with you here. That's why the average ScAmway check is less than ten dollars a month!

I used to be a consultant and major up-line in a multi-level company. Most multi-level people try to go out and sponsor the world (**creating a chain of people**), rather than teaching only 7 recruits to teach 7, etcetera and thereby

COMPOUNDING themselves into a network. If you're involved in a referral plan, this knowledge can transform your life! The bottom line is, build not just **wide**, but also **deep**!

Width, plus **hard work**, on the receiving side of a chain:

Deep plus **less work** puts you on the receiving side of a **NETWORK**:

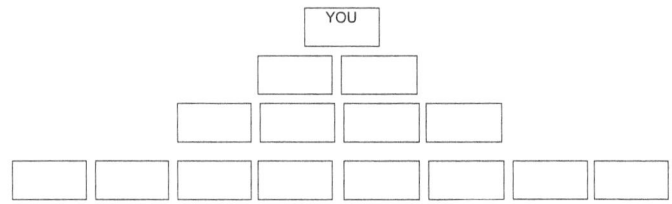

But network marketing still has its pitfalls and is not **The One Perfect Business**. For one thing if you've tried multi-level marketing do you have any friends (who are now ex-friends) you tried to recruit?!!

Oilman J. Pual Getty said you've got to be in a business of your own — it was his first and foremost *"Rule for Success"*. You've also learned that there actually exists a business that is not affected by the long, long list of pitfalls and traps ruining **over 54% of all new small businesses in the United States**!

Where, and what are, these businesses that harness the **FORCE** of compounding? They are literally everywhere in the globe you could travel now, near and far, and high and low. You've touched and been touched by this business but you've never stopped to consider how it could put you on the receiving end of a **powerful** network instead of powering the treadmill running somebody else's money machine!

Let's analyze the receiving end of a network; the person gaining the residual benefits is the one who recognized opportunity before consumers saw the widespread need. **ALL** fortunes are the result of many little residuals flowing into an ever growing pool of money under one person's control.

Larry Page doesn't make 50¢ on every Ad sold: he makes less than 1¢ personally, but with over 12,000,000 accounts pouring money to him day in and day out through Google AdWords, that's $120,000 per day fattening Larry Page's pocket! A bit from a bunch. Just like your bread business we created: lots of people eat your bread and the little bit you earn from lots of people adds up to a lot of dough.

It's easy to imagine yourself building a bread pyramid; the way Dave has of Dave's Killer Bread.

What a powerful idea with solid prospects. But how do you think you'd do building a pyramid around carved Ostrich eggs like those painstakingly carved by Artist Ron at www.wildrosecreations.us. You could be the foremost carved ostrich egg artist, but such specialty products have a high resale value. So you may even have a thriving carved ostrich egg business, but it won't reach NETWORK status.

How many willing and able learners would you have to carve your eggs, and would teach others, and so on? Not many at all.

And of those that would how many could?

The humongous referral based companies (Mary Kay, Avon, Shaklee, Amway, etcetera) have combined revenues in the **BILLIONS** because they deal in basic provisions. Profits come from just a fraction of that revenue.   You may find these businesses distasteful, may not want to have anything to do with them, and may seriously hope that another stranger doesn't try to befriend you to ultimately trick you into joining his or her network.

But those enterprises will pump billions of profits to the benefactors of their networks every day, month, and year forward just like Getty's oil wells. This will happen regardless of you joining or thumbing your nose at them. I can only imagine what you're thinking *"But Shacklee sells vitamins — that's not a basic provision."*

Recent statistics show that athletes and dieters rank vitamins just as important as food!!! Big business deals with basic provisions because everybody needs them making their market vast (the reason oil made J. Paul Getty so rich).

Avon really understands that women need cosmetics, nearly every woman needs cosmetics (except for some of the professors I know in my university economics department), and that they run out of cosmetics. In fact, even during the Great Depression, women still need and used cosmetics! And groceries, too!

CONSUMABLE EXPENDABLE BASIC NECESSITIES BIG BUSINESS MAKES!

OK, there are a few exceptions like the Lava Lamp, Beanie babies, and the Cabbage Patch Dolls. Those businessmen were wise (and **fortunate**) to be on the receiving side of a network **they created** and thrived from for awhile. These are examples of **wealth spurts**, but not **true rivers of money.** J. Paul Getty drilled, pumped, and sold oil, a basic need and continually consumed. Proctor & Gamble controls the lion's share of the grocery store shelf you buy at!

DuPont created the consumable necessity of dynamite and napalm. Ford did, too. When disposable razor blades were invented razor handles were given away free by Gillette. His profit came from the blades (consumable and necessary), **not** the sale of razors.

A modern version of that shrewd business is the computer laser printer. There's very little profit in the printer itself! Why do you think they keep dropping prices on them? That's right — to ultimately sell the printer cartridges which only go up in price!

The Peace Corp became famous for their interview tactics where they would ask candidates to describe a partially filled glass of water.

You may be one of less than 3% of all Americans who see the glass as half full and are appropriately on the receiving side of their networks. As Napoleon hill wrote in Think and Grow Rich, "*Within Every Adversity Lay the Seed of Equal or Greater Benefit.*" Don't worry if you've never seen the glass as half full. This course isn't entitled **How to Master Forex Trading** by accident! This helps you see what you never saw before.

The Buddhists say that *"mystery to a bird is the air, to a fish it's water, and to man it's himself!"*

However there is one aspect of our nature that is not mysterious. Our interdependency means that we **have** to give and receive. And its really a strong intent backing a simple decision to be on the receiving end of wealth that will transform your life for the better.

FIRST SAY TO YOURSELF WHAT YOU WOULD **BE**; AND THEN **DO** WHAT YOU HAVE TO DO. … Greek Philosopher Epictetus, Circa 100 AD.

For FREE Course Audios & Videos Go To

www.TheOnePerfectBusiness.com

You've seen the stories on TV, in the papers, and on the internet where a cancer victim declares, *"This is the best thing that's ever happened to me — I've stopped tobacco, alcohol, and I live every minute of the day to its fullest now. I appreciate my grandkids, kids, wife, and even my dog!*

I used to take all my true blessings for granted, but no more… and all thanks and credit to my cancer!" This is called finding the silver lining.

IT'S NOT WHAT HAPPENS TO YOU, BUT **HOW YOU REACT TO IT THAT MATTERS**…. Greek Philosopher Epictetus, Circa 100 AD.

What motivated your decision to study this course? Maybe you're unemployed, in prison, depressed, bankrupt, in a dead-end job; little do I know, but remember that lemons can be turned into lemonade. Perhaps tragedy wasn't your stimulus to study this course. Maybe you're a lifelong learner looking into a new area… regardless: **EVERY** motivation is swell since it resulted in your study of this course! This will create a new dimension in your life I know it will from all the contented emails in response to this program I receive every month. **How to Master Forex Trading** creates the exit ramp from the rat race, especially yours.

I was working on my doctoral dissertation the day the twin towers came down on 9/11. As I was writing that morning my Russian friend Vladimir called me and we began discussing the situation. Vladimir was a former Soviet Army officer and intelligence expert and I found myself becoming depressed over the whole situation.

If You Enjoy What You Do...

You'll Never Work
Another Day In Your Life!

As we talked, since I had already made up my mind I couldn't write anymore that day — I was in just too lousy a mood and I didn't want all that negativity to spill over into my writing. Then I remembered Think and Grow Rich and thought to myself, *"Where's the equal or greater benefit in this?"*

Just as I was thinking this, Vladimir told me that the Russian military had known for a long time that America had been taking radical religious terrorists too lightly. This is a glaring reminder that religious zealots are different from us. They don't have the same values and don't see things the same way we do. Vladimir went on to list other good possibilities from the attack, let me say without getting into politics or religion that an equal or greater benefit will come of it for all concerned (including the victims). I have never seen the principles Napoleon Hill taught fail ever...

The stories of instant wealth that have captured your imagination are the sensational ones; Google, Microsoft, and Avatar the movie. But these are just a drop in the sea of all of the wealth being discovered now!

OUR GREATEST GLORY

IS NOT IN NEVER FALLING

BUT IN RISING

EVERY TIME WE FALL!

Think of your *"no-brainers"* that, if you would have taken action, would have made you rich…quick. Weren't they out-of-the-box? What we see making the nightly news are out-of-the box (and out of the blue) concepts. BUT FORTUNES FROM THESE ARE NOT MADE! The truly massive fortunes made today are from firms dealing in BASIC CONSUMABLES people need everyday.

Look at Wal-Mart….certainly not a place to brag about shopping! Yet the value of products for Wal-Mart passing through the port of San Diego each year is a larger sum than 93% of ALL countries Gross National Product around the world! **One** company… look at Exxon, Alcoa, United Technologies Corporation, 3M, American Express…American Express? I'll bet you never heard of American Express!

Just kidding!

American Express sells **CURRENCY** for consumable necessities you can't or don't want to pay for right now.   By making currency available to consumers American

Express is directly involved in all BASIC CONSUMABLES — things everyone needs, uses up, and buys again.

Fortunes are being made every day, by thousands of Joe The Plumber types, **AVERAGE** Joes and Jills, whom you'll never see on the **DAVID LETTERMAN SHOW**, the, **OPRAH, DR. PHIL, ELLEN**, or read about in **TIME MAGAZINE**.

The best example of these unspectacular fortunes, only because they become a little more conspicuous are those wealthy families who have sold their local business and the new owner has to introduce him or herself to the local community. Lasting wealth, thusly, is made in enterprises that offer consumers access to goods and services that make modern life possible: **nourishment, shelter, fabric, wheels to work, cellular phones, health care, oil and gas**, and other **need supplying businesses**.

Out-of-the-blue gains come from **INDULGANCE, NARCISISTIC**, or **CRAZE** product businesses. Don't throw out that idea that's been rattling around the back of your brain, though, just put it on the back burner until you've got what it takes to pull it off.

I remember when the nicest golf-course home was sold by my mom in our small community in Northern California when I was finishing high-school. I asked her what business the new buyer owned (the only "*employee*" living in these kinds of homes would be the president of a large corporation!). "*Oh, you know the strawberries in every supermarket in America? His company grows those.*" Another "*basic necessity fortune…*" THINK NEEDS! Ray Bradbury is one of my favorite authors. He laid the truth bare: "*In order to be creative, you don't have to be original.*"

Find a need to supply and you'll find a fortune.

CHAPTER THREE: Learn to Spot Profit Opportunities

So far you've seen that lasting wealth comes from supplying folk's necessities.

And this means controlling your own operation. You need currency (money) to buy the most basic necessities — items everyone consumes, suffers without, **and** purchases time and time again.

THIS MAKES CURRENCY THE MOST BASIC CONSUMABLE OF ALL!

I launched my most profitable business this year (in the past 6 months) and the results so far put every other business I (or you) know of in the dust. I'll start with a business you already know…

Although it's been a *"hot"* topic and blasted all over your internet computer screen, television, radio, newspapers, and magazines since December (2009), you didn't need anybody to tell you that Europe, and especially its PIGS of Portugal, Italy, Greece, and Spain are on very hard times financially. Even shut-ins, with no internet knew this because of the riots people fear may spread to the U.S.

And you know just how serious it is if you've got European friends you email over there. News reports of a rising U.S. Dollar against a falling Euro were everywhere — the Euro is the **CURRENCY** used by people in Europe.

Dollar Strengthens on Greece, Growth Concerns

Wall Street Journal Online

Euro weakens on rate cut evidence

BBC News

Dollar rises, euro weakens

Russia Journal

Daily stories repeated that the global financial collapse in 2009 was being compared to the Great Depression ……………………

No education of **any kind** is required to understand **THE ONE BASIC RULE OF LIFE**: The **LAW** of **SUPPLY** and **DEMAND**. Europe produces cars and America produces cars. If people want European cars more than American cars they will need more Euros to buy the European cars. As they buy more Euros (and sell their U.S. Dollars) the price of the Euro goes up in terms of how many a U.S. dollar will buy.

But this also drives up the price of European cars as the Euro CURRENCY becomes more expensive. They will only pay less than the European dealer's asking price because they can get American cars for less anywhere else. This also drives up America's exports of cars too. This is what makes the world go around — nothing happens until something is sold.

Being more aware and actively looking for profit opportunities now, you speculate: *"Well if the U.S. Dollar is down — way down, it seems reasonable that cheap dollars make exports cheap so demand for U.S. Dollars will **have** to go up, from all the new U.S. Export buying by other countries and with it the price for the U.S. Dollar. That's what the Law of Supply and Demand **requires**!"* You're right! I bet that thought didn't cross your mind when you heard about how weak the U.S. dollar has been.

The U.S. Dollar simply **HAD** to come back up!

So what do you do about it? Open a car dealership? No for not only is that a mentally and physically overwhelming business to get into, but also, the owner of any car dealership won't make a profit on a rising U.S. Dollar. Yeah, he'll be **selling** cars, SUVs, trucks, and vans at higher retail prices, but he would have had to pay **higher dealer prices**! A rise in price doesn't mean a rise in profit.

Well, then, let's think down stream in the supply chain: maybe we should consider opening an automobile manufacturing business like Henry Ford. We would supply many car dealerships with cars, SUVs, trucks, and vans. Since we would be making the automobiles in huge quantities (in order to fill the needs of many individual car dealerships), we would have a lower cost to make each car than any individual dealer could and that difference would be our profit.

Well, I know **I** don't have enough expertise or money to open a manufacturing business, complete with factories and unionized workers; besides wouldn't the cost of steel, copper wires, plastic (from oil), aluminum, and tires (from oil) cost **me**, as a manufacturer, more money too? Sure it would! I would be in the same situation as the car dealer: charging the customer (the grocery stores) higher prices, but having to **pay** higher prices, too.

What's the next step, then?

Who do the manufacturers buy their products from? Well directly from Du Pont, U.S. Steel, Kennecott Copper, and Alcoa Aluminum. But these companies are charging more, as we've already seen, as the higher demand for more commodities, from more demand for more American products like U.S. automobiles — due to rising inflation — is simply passed along.

Who's left? As the U.S. Dollar gets stronger Americans will start to buy more (cheaper) European Automobiles again. Where do Americans get their dollars to buy European cars? That's right — a BANK!

"You mean How to Master Forex Trading was written to tell me to go out, start a bank, and become a banker?!" Although it would be quite profitable to be a banker this year with all the free money Congress is dolling out to banks, what about next year, and the next? Bankers may be starving again next year. Their lives, families, and futures are in banking — **for the long haul**. It's the few *"good"* times like the 2008-2009 bailouts that keep them going. Banking is where some phenomenal

profits are this year, but no, I would never consider being one of America's bankers: it's a thankless business only corrupt top executives come out ahead in. This course opens the door to a bright new world called **How to Master Forex Trading**!

The How to Master Forex Trading Course introduces you to a business that is attracting the brightest minds (you and me included!). It's new because it's not even 50 years old in America.

Is it really possible to begin one's own business with just $1,000, and have none of the swarm of trials and tribulations inherent in any other business anyone knows of? A business that is depression, inflation, and recession proof, with no employees, attorneys, accountants, overhead, licenses, insurance, inventory, marketing, lawsuits, obstacles, or billing?

Yes.

Is it possible to have a business of your own that gives you the prospect and process to amass a **true fortune**, riches above that of ANY OTHER BUSINESS VEHICLE? Yes it is — due to the system of free venture we're blessed with in the good ol' USA.

The governments of the 1st world have promoted the establishment of networks of giant international banks around the globe where importers and exporters can buy and sell currencies used to help Americans have access to all the products they use and need.

Going back to the profit opportunity we spotted in 2009, from which some people lined their pockets with profits. Let's see how we can get into a *"perfect business"* I've been talking to you about:

The Euro trades as a pair against the U.S. Dollar and it was affected by the global economic crisis in 08' and 09.' Let's say we were aware of, and actively looked for, these special profit opportunities in the Fall of 2009 when Europe's problems began making headlines…

This is a graph of the price of the euro that shows the actual, day-to-day, cash on the barrelhead price for the euro currency. For example on February 28, 2010 one euro currency cost $1.36. This is expensive to us but a Dutch family on vacation in Disney World could convert each hard earned euro currency into more than a buck to get a great deal on their food, rides, and fun!

If you're a European tourist on vacation in America you just walk into a bank or an exchange kiosk and buy dollars. If you're the Orlando BMW car dealer, however, you can't afford that lack of planning to pay your German manufacturer when your import invoice comes due. Not only would you fill your bank account with enough Euros to pay all the cars you've sold in U.S. Dollars, but you'd also tell your (international commercial) bank you'll be needing such-and-such an amount next week, next month, and for many months thereafter. You couldn't stay in business otherwise.

To get out of this problem, you can place a **forward** order for currency and use a lay-away plan. Cash prices and forward, lay-away prices may be different. If I'm an importer and sell imports, and I ask you to reserve a certain amount of foreign currency for me which I'll take control of in three months, you're going to ask me for a deposit **and** you're going to charge (or pay) me any interest for the cost to hold in reserve, insure, and maintain my forward order.

Here's a graph of the cash price of the Great Britain Pound (also called the "**cable**") in February of 2010:

Notice that if you'd bought this pair it would have cost you $1.52 per Great Britain Pound.

Currency is priced in PIPs (short for **Price in Points**) out to the fourth decimal and bought (or sold) in 10,000 units. A PIP is at the fourth decimal because very large international banks trade in blocks of 1, 10, or 100 million currency units. This allows the big bank traders to fine tune their trading.

Forex prices are displayed like this;

GBP/USD = 1.5224

This is called a **direct quote** because it's the price of one Great Britain Pound in U.S. Dollars. The PIP is the last digit on the right, so if the market increased by 4 pips the new price would quote as;

GBP/USD = 1.5228

If the market increased by 1,000 pips the new price for the exchange pair would be;

GBP/USD = 1.6224

How to Master Forex Trading was born on August 15, 1971 when the Gold Standard was abandoned for a free floating economy and exchange rates began to fluctuate. Today, the value of a country's currency depends on how much anybody's willing to pay for it. Currency values are **NOT** based on gold reserves. The more in demand a currency is the higher its price and the other way around.

These currency price fluctuations were what the world's largest banks and some large international corporations were hoping for. They quickly began transferring their money back and forth, playing the numbers game, waiting for exchange rates to go down and buying up large amounts of foreign currency to be traded when the rates would come back up. Millionaires and billionaires were made overnight.

They built up the **Foreign Exchange Market (Forex)**.

For years, the Forex market was open only to these large corporations and international banks. They charted the unstable waters of this wide open market system. Eventually, the Forex market grew larger to incorporate all of the currencies of the world, and Forex Trading became a must for any large company.

In 1995, the maturation of the internet allowed the Forex Market to be opened to you and me for the first time — anybody could finally make money on these price fluctuations.   Just two lines on a graph represent each day's fluctuations:

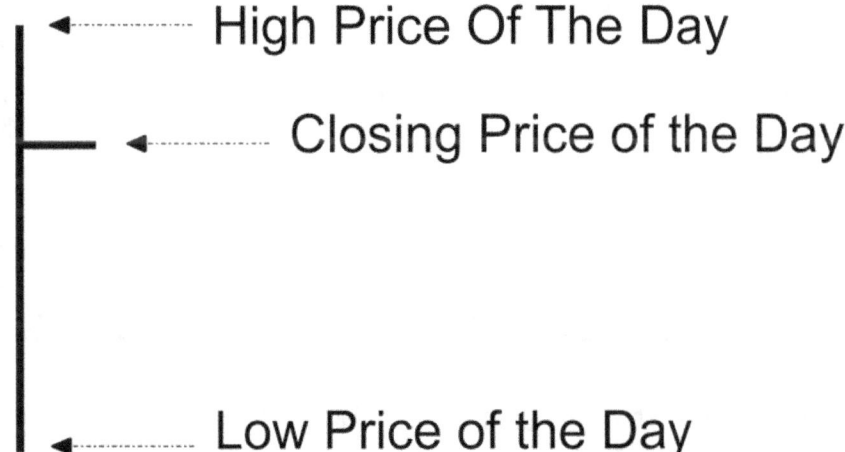

We keep watching the price of currencies *"across the pond"* sensing a profit opportunity as the dollar strengthens against the Great Britain Pound and Euro Currency. Something must be wrong, though — the United States is in an economic depression.

Shouldn't the Great Britain Pound and the Euro Currency be headed higher?

Oh, but there's problems over there too — maybe that's why their currency is sinking in value. The **PIGS** (Portugal, Italy, Greece, and Spain) are in severe production drops and their banks are failing all over the place so it makes sense. I could be wrong, but it makes sense. It's not costing me anything to watch and wait, so I'll keep watching and waiting!

The EUR/USD market has been falling, which means that it costs less in dollars to buy the EUR, but then the price shot up from December 21, 2009 to January 12th, 2010. Maybe this is the profit opportunity I've been looking for.

But now look! Prices shoot straight down from January 12th! My thinking about the U.S. Dollar must have been correct after all.

Price moves like this are what fortunes are made of, but what can I do about the rising value of the U.S. Dollar?!

57

CHAPTER FOUR: A Perfect Business Gone Global

You can invest in the global economy the same way the fortune-builders — the "*big boys*" — do. And this business works anywhere in the world. Suppose you live and work in Europe making money in Euros (I have a **LOT** of students of this course in Europe).

You can decide to open [Insert Your Name] CURRENCY COMPANY by selling (high) 10,000 Euro Currencies at whatever the current price is if you worked and earned your money in Europe. On January 10th, that would have been $1.4514/€. 10,000 Euros at $1.4514/€ is $14,514. You feel the value of the dollar is going higher because of America's increasing exports driving up the DEMAND for American currency. So you see tremendous potential in selling (short) Euros high now, holding on in order to buy them back lower after the American dollar rises further.

Doing this means that you are effectively buying low and selling high.

Isn't this what you do at the gas station? Remember in May of 2007 when a gallon of unleaded jumped to $3.18? Many farms stocked up with extra storage tanks as soon as they heard about the coming gasoline shortage. It's just basic economics — supply and demand. Nothing fancy or sophisticated; requiring neither advanced education (like my Ph.D. in finance), insight, nor computers.

The simple **LAW** of Supply and Demand drives How to Master Forex Trading.

It's one thing, however, to buy a few hundred gallons of gas from a local farm fuel distributor and quite another to sell 10,000 Euros! It's also one thing to **save a few bucks** on a few gallons of gas and another world completely to actually go into the currency business and stand to make literally a **fortune**…

Suppose you even felt secure enough to buy $14,514 by selling 10,000 Euros, where would you hide them all?! That's where the beauty of **How to Master Forex Trading** comes in.

At the world's *"Giant Currency Centers"* you can buy currency on deposit, just like Chase Bank does! That is you can claim $14,514 today (January 10th) for example. But you don't have to do anything with it until you decide to sell it for Euros as your mini-lot specifies! Great! I can buy my American dollars on January 10th, but I don't have to see it, touch it, or deposit it in my personal bank account! And more good news: you only have to put a very small deposit down on your 10,000 Euros worth of American dollars. Your deposit is a miniscule $200. That's all!

Do you recognize the POWER and PROFIT POTENTIAL here? Those of you who are already in business are shaking your heads and muttering. *"No, no, it's too incredible to be true…"* For those of you who haven't yet owned your own business (restaurant, gas station, real estate business, etcetera), let me explain:

COMPOUNDING — LEVERAGE

There are no more powerful principles than compounding and leverage. Suppose you converted 10,000 Euros worth of American dollars and stuffed them under your mattress. As the EUR/USD price drops you buy MORE euros so that you profit like this…

EUR/USD	CURRENT VALUE	€ GAIN ON $14,514
1.4514	€10,000	0%
1.4319	10,136 (€136 gain)	1.4%
1.4288	10,158 (€158 gain)	1.6%
1.4019	10,353 (€353 gain)	3.5%
1.3912	10,433 (€433 gain)	4.3%
1.3621	10,655 (€655 gain)	6.6%

And if you think those Euros are *"funny money"* just take a trip right now — like the month long Mediterranean cruise Marisol and I took last summer. We paid the equivalent of $17 in Euros for a beer, a diet coke, and a little plate of cold-cuts and cheese on a sidewalk café in Cannes on the French Riviera!

You may be thinking, "*Darn I don't live in Europe to make money this way.*"   Here's a secret. With How to Master Forex Trading you can be living in America and do just the opposite. You can sell the high priced Euro today and buy it back cheaper down the road for the exact same profit as above but in American dollars!

If the American dollar strengthens 9¢ to where it's worth $1.36/€, your $14,514 stock of greenbacks you used to control €10,000 are now worth €10,655. You started with €10,000. So that's a €655 gain, or 6.6% profit on your initial investment. If you converted that straight back to American dollars at $1.36/€ you have a $891 profit! Since this gain occurred in two months, your **annual** yield would be 39.6%. Not bad to **protect** your capital and fight inflation, but certainly not enough to begin **accumulating a fortune**!

You now know, however, you can merely invest a SMALL DEPOSIT on this currency. As the exchange rate on the **EUR/USD Forex Trading Pair** drops each American dollar buys **MORE** Euros.   To illustrate, as the EUR/USD Pair drops from $1.4514/€ to $1.4319/€ you **profit** $195 (because $1.4514/€ minus $1.4319/€ equals $0.0195/€ and 0.0195/€ times €10,000 Euros equals $195 American dollars).

$14,514 Converted Back Into Euros

EUR/USD	CURRENT VALUE	$ GAIN ON $200 DEPOSIT
1.4514	€10,000	0%
1.4319	10,136 (€136 = $195 gain)	97.5%
1.4288	10,158 (€158 = $226 gain)	113.0%
1.4019	10,353 (€353 = $495 gain)	247.5%
1.3912	10,433 (€433 = $602 gain)	301.0%
1.36215	10,655 (€655 = $893 gain)	446.3%

That's how fortunes are made! A 446.3% gain on your $200 investment in 2 months equals 2,678% annually!

The **RULE OF 72** illustrates the power of compound interest: divide the constant, 72, by the annual interest any single amount of money earns and the result is how many years needed, on its own, to double.

Take some money earning five-percent annually, through Einstein's miracle of compounding (interest earning interest), and it'll double in exactly 14.4 years (72 divided by 5 = 14.4). That rounds to 15 years. $1,000 deposited and left alone to compound for 15 years at 5% turns into $2,000. A chunk of money earning 8.5% annually doubles about every 9 years (72 divided by 8.5 = 8.47). $1,000 deposited at 8.5% grows to about $2,000 in year nine and $4,000 in 18 years.

At 20% annually a single deposit compounding doubles every 4 years (72 divided by 20 = 3.6 years). $1,000 turns to twice as much at $2,000 by year 4, that turns to twice as many again to $4,000 by year eight, and that replicates by year twelve to $8,000.

YEAR	5%	8.5%	20%
1	$1,000	$1,000	$1,000
2			
3			
4			$2,000
5			
6			
7			
8			$4,000
9		$2,000	
10			
11			
12			**$8,000**
13			
14			
15	**$2,000**		
16			
17			
18		**$4,000**	

CONSERVATION. BUT CERTAINLY **NOT** OPPULENCE!

Now let me analyze your currency business yielding 2,677.8%/year: 72 divided by 2,677.8 = 0.026 years (approximately ten days)…

Year 1 = $200   Year 3 = $259,200   Year 5 = $335,923,200

Year 2 = $7200   Year 4 = $9,331,200   Year 6 = **$12,093,235,200**

A mere $200, through the miracle of compounding grows to $12 **billion** (with a "B)! **That's** how fortunes are built!

 Those of you shaking your heads and sputtering, "*just to good to be true…why isn't everybody doing it?*," are thinking, "*Yes, that's great but what if the American dollar* **weakened***? I could just as easily have* **lost** *$12 billion!*"

How to Master Forex Trading is set up so that you **can't lose** more than the $200 you put into it (unlike commodity trading). Although you could earn 2,677.8%/year in your *"little"* currency business year in and year out, for 6 years, it's not very likely you will. Yet the point is, there's no other business — none — that opens the door to such **leverage**, **compounding**, **power**, and **true fortunes** that this business does. And you haven't seen the best of it!

…*"Lots"* for cash deposit on the worlds strongest currencies can be bought and sold with amazingly little capital — unlike commodity **contracts** these are called **lots** even though the concept is the same.

…Because of the absolute **vastness** of these *"currency hypermarkets,"* you enjoy global **liquidity**: you can buy and sell your lots literally in **seconds**. Just try to get your cash out of an oil well, automobile, tax lien certificate, rental home, real estate flip, McDonald's franchise, or gas station mini-mart business in seconds!

…You can always place a predetermined limit on your risk **at the time you purchase or sell your lots**.

…If you trade through the brokerage, I have pre-screened, for you, you will **not lose more than your initial investment**.

…Your business(es) is under your control at all times which as it should be! You will **never** amass a fortune with someone else managing your money.

…You'll have **none** of the many gut wrenching headaches affecting **all other businesses**!

…As long as people live, breathe, consume goods, and pay for them with freely floating currency, your opportunities for **huge profits** abound.

…Global economic, environmental, social, and political events and the currency fluctuations they cause simply create more **opportunities** for you to profit from!

…As your lots grow in value, they create **internal financing** which can be used to accumulate additional lots and on, and on, and on…

…You can enter and exit your business on a moment's notice, or not at all! And if not, you can create and run an **empire in electronic simulation**! This "*practice to profit*" approach exists in NO OTHER BUSINESS where you can start without risking one red cent. Just **try** to run any business you have in mind in electronic simulation like Nero in the movie, "*The Matrix*" as if the whole business had been perfectly replicated into an Xbox or Play station game… it can't be done! You can merely guess at and approximate what **may** or **may not** be reality in any other business (automobiles, tax lien certificates, rental homes, real estate flipping, McDonald's franchise, or a gas station mini-mart business)! In this business, you can see, plan, practice, and benefit from **real-life events**, not guess work!

"*But isn't this risky,*" people have asked me to whom this is new. Swell. Let's think about uncertainty…

There are a few lucky people who really enjoy their work (and you may be one of them). You're still attached to a single wage — you have no diversification in income. In my MBA finance courses I teach at the University of Puerto Rico I actually show why lack of diversification is dangerous.

Isn't that risky?

Unemployment is at its peak as I write this passage in 2010 sitting at my desk in Northern California. People simply don't look for job security like they used to in the same way people don't look for gold here any more since it's been taken away. Ditto for the nation's pensioners, or disabled! "*My spouse works, too*" you say? Your spouse has to work because inflation has nibbled your wage from a corn cob

64

to a kernel. She has to work to pay the bills because living on your one wage has proven too sketchy!!!

The storm clouds have gathered AND come over the horizon.

"I'm diversified in real estate since my rentals and home are cashed out!" Your own business is different. First of all don't even dare to think of your home as an increasing asset. Your home is your home! It's a roof over your head not another source of additional income! Into foreclosure go over 5,000 homeowners in America every day these days. None of these homeowners thought home ownership was risky before the economy collapsed in 2009. Ask them now. Each one will tell you how risky home ownership is!

Rental houses can kick off great income if the government doesn't flood the market with cheap financing for homeownership. Then all the good tenants stop renting and start buying again. That government mismanagement helped create the most recent real estate market collapse. Or if all the other people *"underwater"* on their loans that have moved in with their in-laws stop flooding the market with *"rentals"* that used to be their homes.

> # World unemployment to stay at 2009 record - U.N.
> ## Reuters, UK
> *"The United Nations agency said unemployment totaled nearly 212 million in 2009, an increase of 34 million over 2007, before the economic crisis."*

And even when rentals were a good business (like way back in the early 80s) about how many hours do your rentals take out of your week? Do you trust the financial integrity of you tenants? Do they care for your properties the way you would? No.

What if your rental(s) was vacant a month, two, or three for the bad economy problems I just listed above? Those payments to the bank go on, and on, and on…

Are you one of the poor souls who got into the real estate business in 2005 just before everybody found out that Wall Street and the bankers had set the market up like dominoes AND given it the final push to collapse? You we're **banking on** the value of your rental(s) to rise weren't you! You were **risking** your money **hoping** rents would rise! Now you've found out just how risky that thinking was! And today, if you haven't already taken tremendous losses, you're wondering if it's worth it — should you try to sell (if you can — the real estate market isn't liquid at all right now!), or refinance at today's rates (if the bank will give you a loan since they stopped lending despite your tax dollar bail-outs!) and pay all those costs on an already *"under-water"* principle balance — owe more than they can be sold for?!

Choices that were safe for your grandfather could be **very risky** for you today.

Did you miss the big real estate boom at the end of the last century and the beginning of the new? You don't trust the market so you're waiting for it to come back up. But if it comes back up aren't you buying too high?

Maybe you jumped into network

Less pay. More hours. Unhappy workers

CNN Money 2010

The majority of those **still employed** now put in longer hours for less pay, quelling motivation in the workplace.

---

marketing and have prospered but how much money and time have you plowed into the *"opportunity?"* How many people do you have to act nice to that you rather not talk to? How many friends have you lost chatting up the multi-level *"opportunity?"* You may not want to stop and think about that one.

And, as I mentioned before if anybody knows this I do!

Good friends are hard to come by … maybe you've learned it's just **too risky** to mix friendship and business. Oh, but you got into that "*no-brainer*" miracle fruit juice multi-level plan? Getting a nice down-line check? Great! I hope you saved all that money because multi-level companies are the most common to go bust or turn out to be scams. Or maybe it seems that the Juice growers got tired of being pushed around and sold directly to the health food stores. All your formally well paying down-lines now get their miracle juice at a third the cost!

I know of a company in Las Vegas that was started by an ex-convict who stole all the money. Multi-level is a hotbed for this kind of activity and it creates nothing but bad press. That puts it out of business even if it gets control back of its juice supply. *"Golly, everything's dicey! I'll keep saving away in a bank savings account!"* That's better than many people do (since so many live hand to mouth these days) but it's **risky**! Banking interest is so low **huge sums** are needed to generate a wealthy lifestyle in a bank savings account, money fund, commercial paper, treasury bills, etc. In fact it literally **takes a fortune to just barely keep a fortune** in any savings account!

> # 24% of Home Mortgages *"Underwater"*
> MSN Money 2010
>
> Here's a sobering number: More than 11.3 million residential properties with mortgages — about 24% of all such properties with mortgages — were "*underwater*" at the end of 2009. That's an increase from over the third quarter and a year ago.

No, if you don't want to end up like the average retiree on $1,705 a month, you'll **have** to act. The only alternative would be to win the lottery or come into an inheritance fortune (as reported in the **Wall Street Journal**).

Preferably, you'll find a business that offers you the most positives with the least negatives. **Without exclusion**, that's the business you're learning in this Course.

This business gives you what you've wanted: endless prospects; self-growth; individual gratification and fulfillment; unlimited room for expansion, both professional and personal; the chance to go at your own pace; to work as you see fit; to contribute to humanity and claim your slice of global wealth. With this business, you can turn your dream list into reality…

On January 10th you decided to open your currency business, knowing that $1,000 is easily a safe amount to "*risk*" on fortune-building, since you know that no fortune has ever been accumulated without at least some risk (and usually a great deal more risk than this currency business requires). You sell one mini lot of EUR/USD which means that you are selling the Euro and buying the dollar — to profit if the American dollar strengthens. Referring to your prior graphs of currency prices you see that the **cash** price was $1.5053 per Euro on December 3rd.

You're not buying with cash, however; you want to merely make a $200 deposit on 10,000 Euros. Once you sell the mini lot you now control 10,000 Euros worth of U.S. Dollars (since you sold the Euros to buy the U.S. Dollars automatically). That's $14,551 dollars. Every PIP the price of the EUR/USD fluctuates means that $1 is added to or subtracted from your $200 deposit. Therefore if the price of the EUR/USD rose 200 PIPs, your $200 deposit would be "*used up.*" If the price of the EUR/USD drops 200 PIPs your $200 deposit has grown to $400.

NO PRICE GOES UP OR DOWN IN A STRAIGHT LINE — IT VARIES, but you're not worried since if the price rises to $1.5253 the special brokerage — I myself use — will shut down the position automatically so that you don't lose more than your initial deposit.

Looking back at the EUR/USD Forex price graph, you see that the price of this pair hasn't been above $1.6020 for over a year; in fact, looking at a 1994-2010 chart the currency pair (where prices have been condensed into a monthly (instead of daily) price fluctuations), you see that the highest currency price was $1.6020 ever, while the lowest price was $0.8230 in 2000!

(SEE NEXT PAGE...)

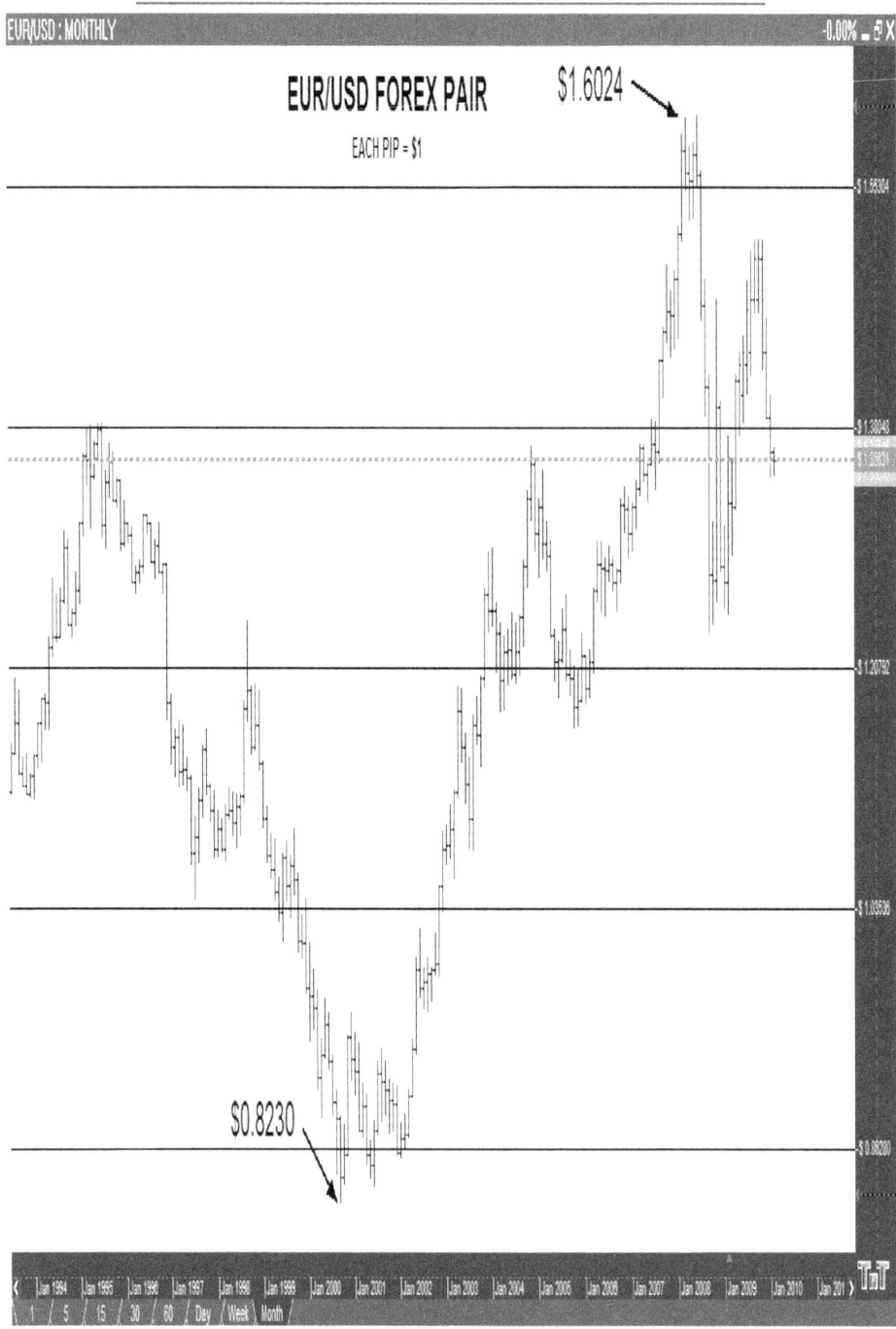

EUR/USD : MONTHLY   -0.00% _ ☐ X

EUR/USD FOREX PAIR

EACH PIP = $1

$1.6024

$0.8230

You check the internet every day and see that the price of the EUR/USD Forex pair is fluctuating (as **always**), but gradually moving lower — which means the dollar is strengthening since the Euro buys less. On January 14th, prices closed at about $1.4511 per Euro. Now your $200 has grown an additional $542 to $742 which would allow you to internally finance another mini lot. Without reaching into your own pocket, without borrowing, without having to qualify. You can instruct that profits be used to add another €10,000 to your *"inventory."*

Should you decide to add another mini lot, each PIP move in the price of the EUR/USD Forex pair will now add or subtract $2 to, or from, your business. You originally invested $200 and now each PIP move — occurring in a micro-second — gives or takes 1%!! You're now at the controls of what Einstein himself considered the worlds most powerful force: COMPOUNDING! You don't have to multiply your business at this point; it's simply another profit opportunity available to you. **You** run **your** own business the way **you** see fit. You could even take your 271% profit ($2,168 annualized!) and close the doors of your currency business if you like.

Suppose you plow the profits back into your business: Now on January 14th you'd have sold **two mini lots** of the EUR/USD Forex pair, the first at $1.5053 per Euro and the second at $1.4511 per Euro. The value of the Euro continues to tumble. Every PIP move is a $2 profit or loss to you. At this point you may want to give instructions that, should the EUR/USD pair climb to 1.4711 to close you out of the market. If that happens you would lose $200 on each mini lot digging into that $542 profit — still leaving you with a $142 profit — or 71% return on the whole deal.

The EUR/USD continues to tumble, your two lots continue to generate profits and on March 1st of 2010 the market closes at $1.3565 per Euro. This is your next opportunity to expand, in fact **double** your business.

Every PIP decrease has generated $2 for your business. The decrease is from $1.4511/€ to $1.3565/€ = 0.0946 or 964 PIPs. 964 PIPs multiplied by $2 = $1,928, just about enough to add 4 more mini lots to your currency business, totaling **six** min lots in all. But that's entirely up to you; you make the decisions. It's **your** business, **your** capital, and **your** decision.

Now that's what I call fast cash!

Notice how you start with $200 but I don't recommend multiplying your business until you accrue $500. This keeps you from multiplying your business too fast. If you've owned a business you probably know that you can go broke if the business is too slow but also if it grows too fast!

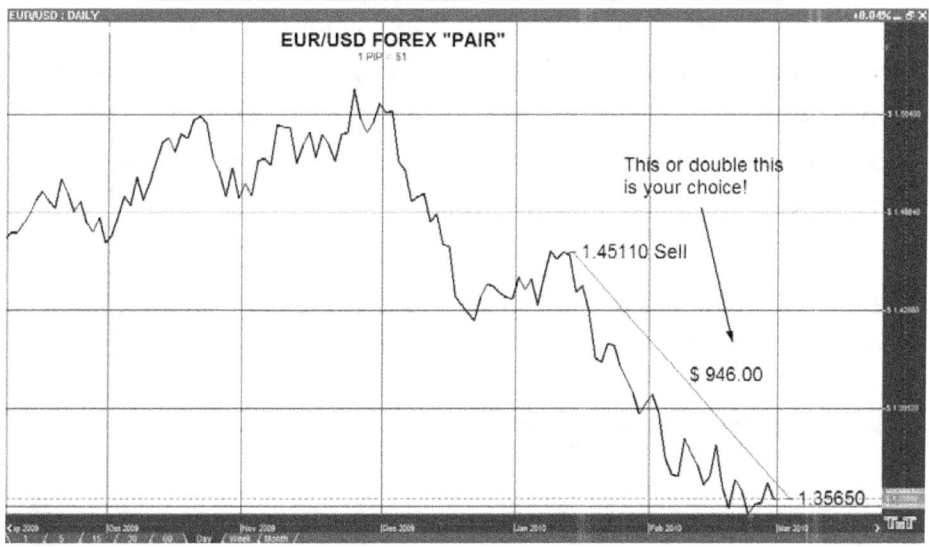

You may also decide to give instructions that, should the EUR/USD pair price rise above $1.3765/€, for example, you want all your min lots (6) sold. Here's how that would look:

12.3.09 sold 1 lot @ $1.5053/€. $200 invested, @ $1.4511/€ =

$542 profit

1.14.10 sold 1 lot @ $1.4511/€.   —0—   , @ $1.4511/€ =

$200 loss

1.14.10 sold 4 lots @ $1.3565/€.   —0—   , @ $1.3765/€ =

$200 Invested

$800 loss

(out of pocket)

(net gain = $688)

But the EUR/USD pair has not risen to $1.3765/€ and you don't have to keep doubling your business as it builds equity. Leverage works **both** ways. Just ask anybody who bought real estate with 5-10% down in 2005 before real estate prices tanked, and who's working a second job to make up the difference between rent received and the monthly payment due!

You Euro currency business has produced such opportunity that you begin to wonder: *"The 2009 economy must have affected more than the Euro currency…"* It did!

Looking at prices for the Great Britain Pound (**cable**) against the U.S. Dollar, we find a very curious situation: (Refer to graph, preceding page).

Just like the Euro currency, this Forex pair trades in terms of how many American dollars and cents one pound will buy. A mini-lot deposit on the pair on March 2nd, 2010 was $200; therefore your $200 controlled 10,000 pounds each worth $1.4960/£ or $14,960. That's about $15,000! How would you like to invest $2,000 to control a $100,000 real estate deal **AND HAVE NO MONTHLY MORTGAGE PAYMENTS OR OTHER OUTLAY?** And if you wanted to sell out, you could simply hit a computer button telling the market, *"sell my property*, please"! It would be

74

sold in a matter of a seconds and any profit from appreciation would go into your account **THAT INSTANT!**

If you sold the GBP/USD pair — remember that means you are selling the pound to buy the U.S. dollar — on January 19th at $1.6357/£, by March 1st the dollar had strengthened to $1.4986/£. That's a 1,371 PIP profit of $1,371 per mini lot on $200 down. That's a 685% return on your investment in 41 days or 6,098% annualized!

If you controlled the equivalent of that $100,000 house — 10 lots for an investment of $1,000 — you'd have a $13,710 profit in just over one month with no contractor problems, realtor problems, appraiser problems, tenant problems, or bank problems!

Again, that's a 685% return on your investment in 41 days or 6,098% annualized! I know a commercial advertising *"Our bank actually helps you get what you want"* What I want? It can't even **approach** those last three **digits**! Do you want to amass a fortune? A **modest** amount of capital, time and study, while paying attention open your door to How to Master Forex Trading.

You need to risk money to make money? Rubbish. In this business there's no need to risk your home or your retirement savings. And you don't need a license, test, or a degree. And you never have to turn your back on your family.

In fact you can learn this business with less than the time it takes you to watch your favorite TV show before you've ever pulled your $1,000 capital out of your wallet. Silent fortunes are earned worldwide by thousands of people. You'll never hear about these experts, they're never on the **ELLEN SHOW**.

These people aren't on TV infomercials, they don't give seminars, they lives of leisure and don't need anybody apart from the love and support of their immediate family.

What other ways does the U.S. dollar fluctuate? How about when it was weakening? Let's see…

From January 1st, 2002 to July 1st of 2008 the U.S. Dollar weakened against the Euro. The EUR/USD Forex Pair climbed from $0.8537/€ to $1.5586/€. That massive PIP increase represented a $7,049 profit per mini lot on a $200 deposit. That's a 3,524% return in 6 ½ years or 542% annualized! Who ever heard of getting 3,524% return on your money?!

If you harness the internal financing opportunities the EUR/USD presented, this could have happened:

With a $200 mini lot deposit each 500 PIP upward movement would allow a mini lot to duplicate itself:

			Value at 1.5586
1 lot @	$0.8537/€	$ 200.00	$ 7,049.00
1 lot @	0.9037	— 0 —	$ 6,549.00
2 lots @	0.9537	— 0 —	$ 12,098.00
4 lots @	1.0037	— 0 —	$ 22,196.00

76

8 lots @	1.0537	— 0 —	$ 40,392.00
16 lots @	1.1037	— 0 —	$ 72,784.00
32 lots @	1.1537	— 0 —	$129,568.00
64 lots @	1.2037	— 0 —	$227,136.00
128 lots @	1.2537	— 0 —	$390,272.00
256			$908,044.00

Pie in the sky? Did somebody pull this off? ABSOLUTELY! HUNDREDS, PERHAPS THOUSANDS, EARNED NEARLY A MILLION DOLLARS IN JUST OVER 6 YEARS, USING JUST $200 SAFELY AND PRUDENTLY!

What if you'd earned just a **fraction** as well? A tenth is $90,044. Can you do 1/10th as well with forethought, simulated practice, a little thought, and some action?

Can you recognize the concept at work here? Can you see why this course is titled **HOW TO MASTER FOREX TRADING**?

The same price action, leverage, and a little time turned $200 for one mini-lot of Forex into nearly a **MILLION DOLLARS**!!! The only thing changed is how you **use** the concept. A large wave will support ten surfers as easily as it will support one — the wave is so big and powerful it feels nothing. It's up to you entirely, the very same $200, 6 ½ years, and planning that resulted in $7,049 could have produced nearly a million dollars! **This silent force is omni-present**; your use is your decision.

The thought may have come to you, *"If I'd only seen this before…there may be no major price moves for many decades to come.."* IT MATTERS NOT! SUCH PRICE MOVES HAPPEN EVERY YEAR **A COUPLE OF TIMES AT LEAST**! You prosper by knowing what you are looking at and understanding the action you must take!

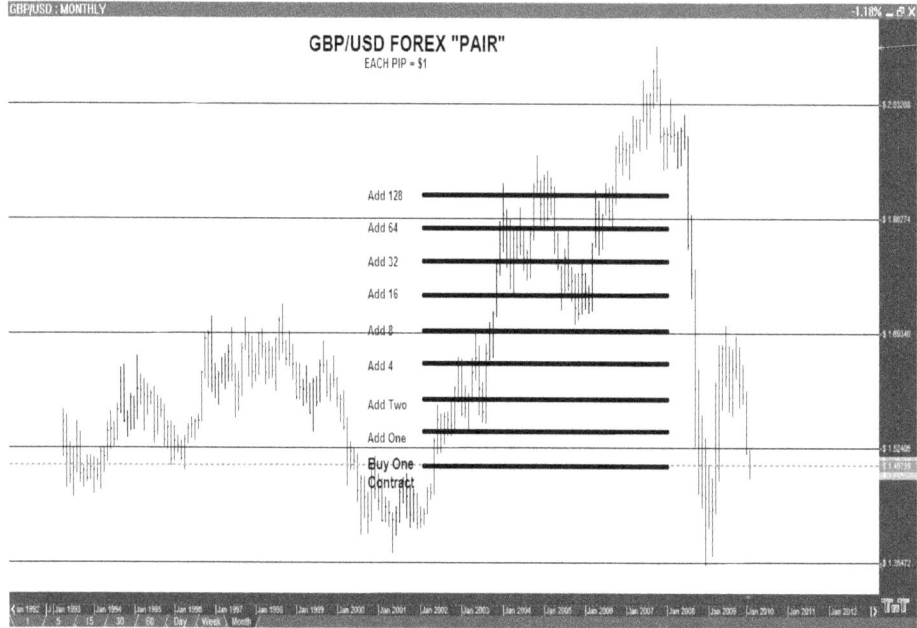

From May 1st, 2002 through October 1st, 2007, the Great Britain Pound
strengthened against the U.S. dollar. The deposit on a £10,000 mini lot was $200
(oop…I mistakenly called is a "*contract*" in the chart above because of my years of
futures trading) the market moved up 5,812 PIPs, generating a $5,812 profit in just
over 5 years, or 2,906%.

How could the silent force be employed here?

If the Pound Sterling is affected by the U.S. Dollar's fluctuations, wouldn't the New Zealand Dollar be affected too!

From March 9th, 2008 through March 1st, 2009 the New Zealand Dollar weakened against the U.S. Dollar. With a mini lot deposit of $200, every 500 PIP movement would have allowed you to internally finance more mini lots. How many would you have held, and what would your profit picture have been on March 1st?

Never even heard of the **Turkish Lira**? It trades against the U.S. Dollar as **USD/TRY** in terms of how many Liras a dollar can buy.   This is called an indirect quote since it's backwards from the usual — remember that the Euro Currency trades as the foreign currency first in EUR/USD. But what really interests me is that I could have turned the explosive move in July of 2008 ($3,724.50 for a single mini lot) into a **major** profit opportunity yielding **hundreds of percents** in four short weeks.

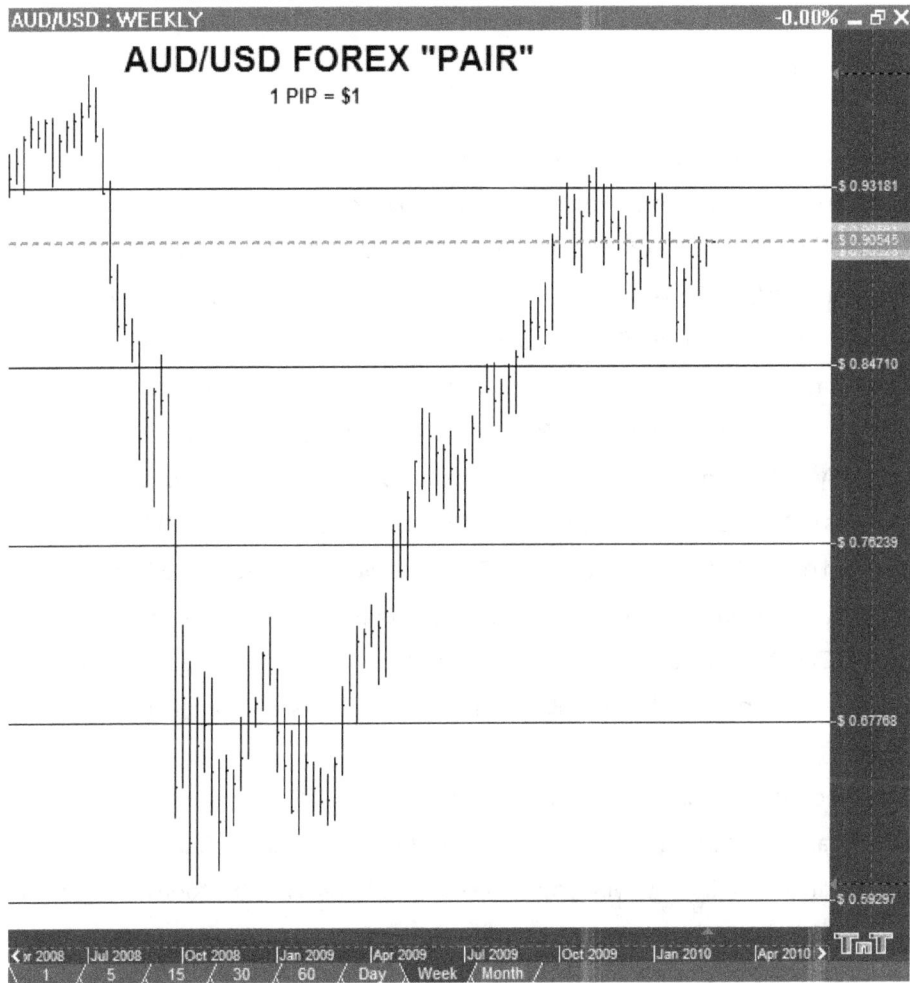

Well at least you've **heard** about the Australian Dollar. Which was a sensational business opportunity for many, many investors from October 2008 to October 2009. Replace the AUD/USD label above with any other pair of currencies you can think of from any country with a safe political economy — would it really **matter**?

Not to a student of this course…

Your right to wealth isn't just perfect…it's indispensable. This business deals in the one universal necessity — MONEY — that buys the things people must have in order to live. Your business will never run out of *"customers,"* unless the world runs out of floating money!

Where did you wake up today? Was it in a tent (many people are these days because of the banks), camper, motel, hotel, apartment, condominium, or a house? Was it built of FABRIC, LUMBER, PLYWOOD, PLASTIC, or DIRT, TIRES, and OLD CANS? Was it powered? Then COPPER carried electricity to it. You turned the lights off and on with SILVER in the switches. Did it have a view? The window frame was likely made of ALUMINUM. Was it a cold winter day? It was undoubtedly warmed with NATURAL GAS or HEATING OIL either directly or indirectly. When you used your computer did you know that the mother-board contains GOLD? Did you exercise? You probably wore COTTON or CRUDE OIL in the form of synthetic or natural fabric. Did you have COFFEE for breakfast? Do you put SUGAR in your COCOA instead? Did you eat oatmeal which is a GRAIN PRODUCT? Did you eat bacon or a breakfast steak? These are HOGS and CATTLE meat. I always have ORANGE JUICE at my mother in-laws with breakfast…

Did you drive to work? It was likely fueled with GASOLINE. Maybe you're a skateboarder… it uses rubber tires. Did you check INTEREST RATES to see how bond market is doing? Maybe you checked the STOCK INDEXES today to see how your 401(k) plan is doing when you got to work this morning?

All of these primary producer products make up BASIC COMMODITIES that radically impact our quality of living. Many people have businesses in these markets. At one time people thought this was a "perfect" business but there is a serious flaw to overcome in **trading commodities**. You can lose **more** than you invest — a lot more!

The Forex market fixes this flaw with the **NO NEGATIVE ACCOUNT BALANCE GUARANTEE** at the special brokerage I myself use to trade these markets.

CHAPTER FIVE: Daily Life Creates Global Profit Opportunities

Webster's says *"Forex is short for Foreign Exchange."* Then it defines Foreign Exchange as, *"the system by which one currency is converted into another, enabling international transactions to take place without the physical transportation of gold."* That covers EVERY good and service in our material world!

In fact, isn't **everything you do** based on the flow — the export and import — of goods and services? And that flow of goods and services affects the supply and demand of foreign currencies used world wide to exchange all those imports and exports. Supply and Demand… It's been observed that *"nothing is more constant than change."* Our world markets are in perpetual flux. This flux can be graphed making evident the change in supply and demand. You've already seen how price changes are documented in the Forex markets.

Commodity Exchanges (*"giant supermarkets"*) offer businessmen an orderly transfer of commodities between buyer and seller. They come from as far back as medieval France and England, yet the oldest in the New World was in Chicago in 1848. Futures contracts originated in the 1860's that guaranteed the price primary producer received for folks like grain farmers. This guaranteed the price another company in the supply chain would pay — like Kellogg's when they buy to make corn flakes. This also guaranteed the price Kellogg's would have to pay. And protected both parties in the contract; the supplier from price decreases and the buyer from price increases.

Before 1971 all world currencies were fixed in price by the Breton Woods system.

This made imports and exports easy for Kellogg's. They could just ship their Corn Flakes overseas to importers and easily convert the currency back at the fixed price when the invoice came due overseas. After 1971 the Bretton Woods system was dismantled by President Nixon and all currencies were forced to fend for themselves by freely floating against one another. The massive international banks — these are so big they won't even let you or I through the front door with a million dollar bag of cash to open a deposit account — created currency exchange desks to help their large corporate clients deal with the additional risk of currency price fluctuations. A change of the value of currencies could easily devalue Kellogg's export invoices by the time the importer had to pay.

And since exchange rates now freely floated, the invoice the importer had to pay could just as easily increase in cost!

Over time currency trading focused into 3 major cities that were well located around the globe to allow for 24 hour trading; New York, London, and Tokyo. By acquiring an office building in these three cities a massive international bank like Chase Bank could have employees buying and selling currency forward to lock in foreign currency rates for the importing and exporting activities of their large corporate clients.

This is very different than in the futures industry where anybody can buy and sell contracts on commodities.

Only the largest corporate clients, their international commercial banks, or well-capitalized former commercial bank traders — who left and started currency hedge funds — could buy and sell currency forward contracts in the **interbank forward market**. This was not only because no brokers for the public existed but also because the lot sizes are humongous; 1,000,000 currency units is a *"mini"* in the interbank market and 10,000,000 is *"standard!"* But as the internet grew and became faster and more efficient a whole new possibility came up.

Some enterprising brokerages came up with the idea of creating a cash market that shadows the interbank forward market. This is just like off-track horse race betting where bets never go through the big race track. This has worked very well because the interbank market is not regulated by any government.

By keeping all the money in the network of cash Forex brokers AND using the power of the modern computer you can achieve 4 to 8 times the leverage of commodity trading PLUS rest assured that you won't lose more than your initial investment.

Many former futures traders have switched over to Forex trading for four major reasons:

1. Quick, efficient, and low cost.
2. World-wide, free market price statistics.
3. To capitalize on the profit producing trends inherent to currencies.
4. To trade in an environment where losing more than your investment is not possible (through the special brokerage account in the Track n' Trade Program).

The Forex exchange doesn't exist in one single place. It's a network of computers and trading desks connecting the entire globe! This is another advantage because you don't have to pay fees to the CFTC or NFA as you would in the futures markets; don't worry if you don't understand this. You can even open an account in England to guarantee the U.S. government won't meddle in your Forex trading.

This market is dedicated exclusively to speculators. Speculators are folks who buy and sell currency contracts because they expect to profit by forecasting price changes. Who are these speculators, anyway? They **rarely use** the currencies they trade. Studies from major schools indicate that most Forex traders are ordinary like you and me with a small amount of capital to risk on a business of their own. Also revealed is that these traders have no special knowledge of the currencies they trade and come from diverse occupations: Farmers, salesmen, teachers, attorneys, secretaries, clerks, prisoners, doctors, mechanics, retirees, ranchers, any and all!

No "*normal*" profile exists!

These folks, who are the major reason Forex trading is exploding in record breaking rates, even as the stock market slumps, far overshadowing the New York Stock Exchange or Chicago Board of Trade's growth statistics, come for the **many vital advantages** the Forex markets offer.

You might be thinking, "*If this is so fantastic why have I heard that Forex is so risky?*" because the source of this is that you, and 95% of the other persons in the world, have been handicapped by the vast network of propaganda, hear say, deceit, misinformation, and non-information that smothers the truth. Let's remove each one at a time.

"MOST PEOPLE LOSE EVERYTHING IN FOREX"

True! If you mean by losing everything as "*only what you put into it.*" Commodity trading is somewhat similar, and the Federal regulator, the Commodity Futures Trading Commission (CFTC) doesn't and never has reported official statistics on this, but it's generally accepted that between 75% and 95% of all commodity traders lose money — Forex statistics are similar. Rubbish! That should be stated "*75-95% of all Forex traders turn their money over to internet robots programmed by con-artists who charge them for bogus settings that proceed to trade their money away.*"

Ask anybody who lost money in Forex **exactly** what occurred....

You'll get no response because s/he doesn't **even understand** what occured! You'll hear a response along these lines: "*Oh, I don't know. I saw this internet advertisement for a Forex robot 'guaranteed' to make me rich. All I had to do was open an account and turn it on. Then, a week later, it had me in Euros, the Pound, the Swiss Franc, the Canadian Dollar, and the Yen. It happened so fast I didn't know what was happening!*"

If you were in the market for good business would you walk into a commercial real estate office and ask for somebody who will do it for you completely (just as these Forex trading robots being unscrupulously promoted by clever internet marketers are supposedly able to think for you)? Would you hand over a check for thousands with the instructions, *"Get out there and find a great deal for me in a Laundromat, or other business"*? I'll check in on you now and then.

Absurd!

ARE YOU FOOLISH ENOUGH TO BELIEVE THIS?

100% No Loss Robot
The original fully automatic no loss robot! Only $199!

Details   Buy Now

Sadly, Many Are!

If the agent knew of a truly good deal and had the knowledge to do it like that they'd just snap it up for themselves. So anybody that would take your money under those terms would be untrustworthy by virtue of saying yes.

But that's exactly how *"investors"* lose money in the Forex markets! Even in Vegas you've got to know the basic rules of the game! Obviously anybody entering these markets in such an unsafe way would call Forex "***terrifying***" and "***deathly!***"

THE HOW TO MASTER FOREX TRADING program will teach you to recognize, unique money-making situations, yet these opportunities don't pop up every day, week, or perhaps monthly. You must quietly and pensively hunt, aware that these opportunities do arise, year to year, faithfully — **BUT YOU MUST PATIENTLY PREPARE AND STALK THEM.**

I am a research partner and friend with prestigious University of South Carolina professor Dr. Eric Powers who earned his Ph.D. in finance from the Massachusetts

Institute of Technology. Eric has one of the most pleasant personalities of anybody I know — especially for somebody so darn smart!

Whenever I get upset from bad research results or a rejected academic finance article he always say's, *"Glass half empty… or half full?!"* then he sits back and grins at me till I start grinning too.

So what about the glass half empty view that 75% to 95% of all people lose everything they put into Forex? That means that for every 3 losers 1 gets to win the entire loser's money or that for EVERY 19 LOSERS ONE GETS RICH!

What if, just think what if, you actually learn the rules and practice first, then wait and plan to become one of the 25-5% who **WIN EVERYTHING** from the 75-95% who lose!!!

Professional traders on the big interbank foreign exchange trading desks are in Forex to make a living — it's their **job**. The same as it's a Las Vegas dealer's job to play cards. If you sit at his/her table, you must play or you'll be asked to leave. I approach Forex the same way: don't sit down until you know what you're doing. And don't sit down before you're ready to play. Most Forex *"traders"* (gambling fools) open a Forex account with too much money (because the robot they bought for $19.95 on the internet either recommended or required a certain, high amount — just like the $100-minimum-bet poker table in Las Vegas) and the Forex robot manual says, *"Ok, you've come to play the market, let's get going!"*

It creeps up on you (Wasn't it you who was supposed to be in charge?) that the robot is buying and selling lots for you! Right now (and better yet yesterday) I want you to become — AND YOUR SUCCESS IS AS SIMPLE AS YOUR DETERMINED DECISION TO DO SO — one of those 5-25% who silently trade out of public view, those who CONSISTENTLY MAKE A LIESURE LIFE STYLE IN FOREX TRADING! THE HOW TO MASTER FOREX TRADING program is the very best beginning I know of.

"IN FOREX IT TAKES MONEY (PILES OF IT) TO MAKE MONEY."

Untrue!

It's not money making money in Forex...your mini lots make you money. You'll get experienced first with **one mini lot** and let that **little soldier of fortune** go to work **for you**. Deposits on lots (called *"Margin"*) are the same across all pairs in Forex. The brokerage I use, charges $200 margin per Forex mini lot AND NO COMMISSIONS! That's because this brokerage only charges you the difference between the selling (asking for price) and the buying (or bidding) price— called the spread. This makes the cost of trading even cheaper than the supposedly low commissions the online stock brokerages charge!

Some Forex brokerages will require you to open your account with more than $1,000. It's not unusual for some Forex brokerages to ask, or require, you to establish an opening margin account of $10,000, $20,000, or more! Don't give your business to bad brokerages, there are **plenty** to chose from — and the best is the one I use — easily opened from the trading platform I also use (go to http://www.thebestbusinessonearth.com/ now for your FREE trial).

I've learned that IF YOU CAN'T PROSPER IN FOREX with $1,000, YOU CAN'T SUCCEED WITH $5,000 OR $25,000, OR EVEN $125,000! Remember that, freind! I believe that those starting to trade Forex with gobs and gobs of money do **horribly** because **their perspectives change**. You've seen the *"high rollers"* blow through small fortunes in Las Vegas casinos...that's the *"What Happens In Vegas, Stays In Vegas"* experience I'm talking about here. If you (could) observe successful Forex traders, you'd witness them build a small pile of cash into a big one, remove most of the new pile, AND BEGIN AGAIN. The bottom line, and answer to this question, is what I've taught throughout my career as an MBA finance professor: SELF-ENRICHMENT.

No one (Or no-robot) has, **or will ever**, handle your money as well as you will! SELF-ENRICHMENT IS THE **ONLY** METHOD TO BUILD GREAT AND LASTING WEALTH. Business managers (and owners) running a McDonald's franchise (I say this with reservation) handle fortune preservation with moderate mediocrity, but WEALTH-BUILDING IS IN YOUR HANDS — WHERE IT SHOULD BE!

"FOREX IS FOR EXPERTS — OF THIS I KNOW NOTHING!"

Remember the few traders in the winner's circle? Those 5-25% of people who do this are ORDINARY FOLKS who started with SMALL AMOUNTS! Who do you think knows more about currencies than people who use them to live day to day? Recently the worst traders have been revealed lurking behind trading desks of the largest international banks. Evidence — hard facts — shows us that *"only the insiders make money in Forex"* Is absolute utter rubbish. If this were true the big banks would never have had to have been bailed out by the US Government — and the Forex market would then be non-efficient, un-tradable, and un-profitable! Not only has that not the case… the **reverse** has happened.

Don't worry about sophistication, the simplicity of the Forex market will astound you. You need an ample vocabulary in the stock, bond, and financial markets. But a new language is absolutely unnecessary to run your own successful currency business. You're learning all the volcabulary you need to know throughout this program. It's more than enough to hold your own in any Forex discussion.

Don't feel inferior!

It really is just YOU against the vast currency market. There's nobody *"out there to get you!"* The Cosmos doesn't know you any more than the market, but you could choke in either one. If you've choked before, it was your **lack of understanding through diligent preparation, that's all,** nothing more. Here you learn the foundations of trading success THAT WORK, and will put you well above the other 75-95%!

As you become more and more involved in this business, you'll be exposed to varied services, software, systems, and options, but it all boils down to one thing: HOW TO SUCCESFULLY OPERATE ON YOUR OWN. You'll find, as you move forward, that the methods for running your own Forex business in HOW TO MASTER FOREX TRADING to be the simplest, easiest, most sound, and most successful. Nothing is 100% in life. And nobody is offering any guarantees: it's discretion and discipline that builds lasting wealth and that's what this course teaches effectively. As you may be tempted in the future to act on some new fad in technical analysis, fundamental craze, or *"foolproof,"* sure-thing Forex robot or trading system, keep this in mind about what you're learning here: DON'T FIX WHAT ALREADY WORKS!

"ISN'T THE MARKET CHOCK-FULL OF COMPETITORS?"

Forex trading is a competition between you, the market, and nobody else! Not only is nobody out there competing with you but this also means only you will come out on top if you set your mind to it! The Forex market's amazing liquidity is proof that these activities are not competitive. *"Competition"* means you couldn't buy or sell mini lots when you wanted to for a profit, but that's simply untrue here. You can (and will) hit the button on your computer keyboard, and buy or sell in a **fraction of a second**. Then there has to be someone else, somewhere else on the globe who has (or wants) what you're selling or buying. For every mini lot bought (expecting the base currency to rise), somebody else must wish to sell (expecting the base currency price to drop).[1] The vast Forex markets make pairing up buyers and sellers no problem.

"I HEARD THE FOREX MARKET IS A FRAUD?!"

---

[1] The **BASE CURRENCY** is always the first in the pair. It's the EUR in the EUR/USD Forex *"Pair."*

Most everybody cheers for a rising stock. Few sell short (expecting prices to drop). But with Forex we've seen that nearly half of investors expect prices to rise (they're "**long**" or "**bullish**" the base currency) and nearly the other half are "**short**" or "**bearish**" the base currency.

What's more just than that?

Merchants will always have buyers of foreign currency to fuel world trade, but the stock market often has nobody buying…only sellers. Forex markets are fundamental, with an unambiguous hard cold **cash value**…in fact you here you can name your cash; euros, pounds or sterling. Stocks have no real value other than what somebody else is willing to pay. Therein lies the fundamental difference between these two capital markets. I prefer operating in Forex because I can use currency to buy food, shelter, fun with my wife in any part of the world, but what can I do with a share of stock? When companies go bankrupt some people use their share certificates to cover their walls when they can't afford wallpaper…

In addition to the many fail-safes programmed into the electronic Forex markets, the US government watchdogs strict rules in the same way it does with any other capital market. It's illegal, for instance, for your Forex clearing firm to charge an artificially inflated spread to force you to pay more than you owe to run your business.

There possibly is a dangerous situation in the Forex markets you should know from the start: FOREX BROKERAGES EXIST TO EARN LIVING, PLAIN AND SIMPLE. The broker isn't a competent Forex trader or s/he would be operating his or her own currency business! I admire these brokers for the service they perform (I wouldn't consider that line of work!), but you must realize where their money comes from, it comes from the spread you pay for each and every mini lot you buy and sell. The brokerage doesn't care if you made money or lost money. That doesn't matter. What only matters to them are how many times you buy and sell mini lot(s).

Many Forex brokerages don't care if they keep or lose your business. Most Forex brokerages are on-line, so it really doesn't matter what country in the world they're located in. What does matter is that your orders are efficiently executed. You don't want advice from your broker, you don't need a shoulder to cry on, or someone to congratulate you; all you need is a connection between YOU and the FOREX MARKET, AND THAT'S ALL!

Today, we're all able to sit at a little home computer and punch in our orders. Now all you need is a great trading platform and an online brokerage (that allows you to trade directly without ordering through a broker) based on high standards of integrity — both of which you can get here…
http://www.thebestbusinessonearth.com/

"I'M BUSY AND CAN'T BE GLUED TO THE COMPUTER SCREEN!"

If you thought this I bet you already are trading Forex, or maybe you used to trade futures contracts! And with all due respect I reckon you're a **loser** in the markets. It's unnecessary, AND UNSENSIBLE, to keep a constant watch on the price fluctuations in Forex. You'll soon learn how to recognize profitable plays, develop a solid, clear-cut operating plan, enter the market, react to spot your opportunity, create a sound, simple business plan; establish your position in the market; and provide for eventualities. Then you can live in Europe with an internet connection (or just cruise an entire month as I did last summer in the Mediterranean starting from London!) for six months or an entire year and never check the website, listen to a radio, watch a TV, or make a phone call!

Sure, like myself, you'll probably want to check your trading platform once a day, but its unnecessary! Ask anybody you know who operates a business how stressed they'd be not checking in for a long time: *"NOT POSSIBLE!"* You'll hear. *"If I didn't call, thre'd be nothing to come back to!"* Another basis for why this is How to Master Forex Trading.

You just thought, *"THERE'S NO TIME IN MY SCHEDULE!"*

There's no time? There's no time like now to get going in this business. Would you agree that the GBP/USD example you've already seen could create at the very least a small fortune?   It would take you working your day job over 20 years, to accomplish what the EUR/USD did for many traders in a **few short years**!

We've all got the same amount of time in a day; it's what we do with our time that counts. There's never a time problem; what many people have is a **focus** problem. The traders operating businesses on the EUR/USD move **couldn't have spent two hours a day if they tried!**

ISN'T THIS ANOTHER "*THROW-THE-DICE*" GAMBLE?

For those who lose money (75-95% it surely is), but it not for you. What would it be like to own a 21 table in Las Vegas? Now that's a profitable **operation**, isn't it? Is the magnificent Bellagio hotel and casino is a **gambling** business?

No way!

Such hotels and casinos were built around sound business practices — just as your Forex business will be. In fact, imagine a better than a 70% success rate if you plan carefully and follow the guidelines in this **program** with discipline.

I know of no other venture requiring such little investment, with such a high potential reward. You could get into something with near certain success by purchasing a McDonald's Franchise, and do you have the **$950,200-$1,800,000 (yes, million) cash,** and yet it's four out to six years to recover your money? Let's say you've got the wherewithal to do it, such a franchise couldn't give you the possibilities your currency business will! And could you pick up and move to the Costa del Sol in Spain anytime you wish…or anywhere else in the world with high-speed internet (which now is most of the world)? No way. Ponder this a bit … close these pages and think.

■■■■ **THINK NOW THEN CONTINUE** ■■■■

Understand now why this course is, "How to Master Forex Trading?"

Losses will occur in your Forex business. Nothing (not even McDonalds) is 100% guaranteed. In fact, you could experience losing trades nearly five times out of ten, but those five profitable ones will probably more than outweigh the losses because you can't lose more than your $1,000 capital!

Let's play a game? Imagine a hundred quarters you control and a hundred silver dollars I control. After a flip I win if both land heads up. But, when both land tails up you win. Want to play?

If you know math you will with a loud "*yes*!"

We'll each win half the time.

However you lose ¼ of what I lose and you win 4 times what I win! This is what I am teaching you to do in the Forex markets. Believe me when I say such opportunities are there… I just turned a $500 account into $5,214 in less then 6 months to prove a point to my MBA students. It paid for my European cruise this summer visiting such places as Cannes, Rome, Venice, and Corfu!

All that's required is that you monitor, stalk, strategize, and take action with what you learn here. When you do recognize the time to take action, you claim How to Master Forex Trading — bar none — positioned to reap profits you've likely scarcely dreamed of.

Spotting and acting on just one of the several (or many) **special circumstances** that percolate each and every year may build a money machine so grand and fruitful that you may *"stop working"* for quite a while — years possibly — the likelihood is low that you'll "*retire*" however. I know of no wealthy trader who has taken their leave of **The One Perfect Business**. Those who curl up into a sedentary ball on the couch at retirement wither and die soon… that's well known. The ones who have a bucket list after retiring from their former "*career*" are the ones who thrive!

Nevada Security Bank ran a series of TV commercials in California that should never have been allowed on the public airwaves. They pictured various folks in their *"sunset years"* celebrating after watching a discussion of a bad economy followed by the banks "*solution*." The message to these senior citizens was, *"Oh, no. I can't start something new in this risky economy, I should hide my head in the sand and accept this bank's High Five 1.85% CD."*

WHAT A DESTRUCTIVE PIECE OF YELLOW "JOURNALISM!" How many of our needy elderly have been sucked in by such fetid rubbish? I wonder how many, on the verge of discovery of something great, pulled back into the relative darkness of their familiar homes (cages) and kept trifling around?

None of them stopped to check the FACT that inflation at the time was 2.66% meaning that their return on these CDs was really -0.81% (YES, THAT'S NEGATIVE)! NOW THAT'S WHAT I CALL RISK — TRUSTING A BANK! I trust that many came to the same conclusion, closed their savings accounts, and sent a severe letter illuminating why.

I built our wealth protecting our cash reserves.

That's why I never want you to risk more than $1,000. And I never want you to invest with an ongoing negative return. Nevada *"Security"* really went too far.

They act like it's a hair cut when it's really a beheading! Here we arrive once again at the flawlessness of How to Master Forex Trading: you don't need to debt-lock your home, borrow money, or decimate your cash savings to start a business — a mustard seed of a business with the prospective to become a massive operation!

"BUT IF I DON'T HAVE TWO PENNIES TO RUB TOGETHER?"

What a **stroke of luck** that you've decided to read this course right now since you've been barking up the **wrong tree**. To receive you must first give (in this case your time of study). This is an immutable law of this universe of time and space we inhabit. Napoleon Hill termed this use of your right to chose *"definiteness of purpose."* If something is of adequately high utility to you success will come from your definite decision to put the most powerful force in creation to work for you — your mind — to inspire a solution! In fact, Hill emphasized that, *"what the mind can conceive and believe, it can achieve."*

Watch this video now: http://www.youtube.com/watch?v=2hA-7aq6OXI

THINK about every time you've really wanted something that you considered difficult yet easily achieved. Wasn't your success initiated by a direct and definite decision quite different from deciding what color of socks you'll wear tomorrow morning? This ability creates lasting wealth as easily as small successes since its power is beyond time and space! Read and listen to "THE RICHEST MAN IN BABYLON" by George S. Clason which you can get at Amazon.com in both book and audio format:

Audio Book Here: **http://tinyurl.com/39fr3l4**

Listen to that masterpiece for a week or so driving to work! You'll discover how simple it truly was for the richest man in Babylon to arrive!

I write this at a poignant time in world history. It's 2010 and we face the worst depression since 1934. You may be living in a tent camp in Sacramento because you lost your job, your home, and your former life. You may have gone from middle management to bagging groceries. But if you harness How to Master Forex Trading you may decide to buy the grocery store next year!

"THIS SOUNDS TOO GOOD TO BE TRUE... A 70% ODDS OF SUCCESS SEEMS TOO HIGH...HOW CAN YOU JUSTIFY THIS?"

The price of any currency can be simplified to mathematical probability. Your life insurance company reduces your entire life to the chances of your kicking the bucket today, tomorrow, or in twenty five years and three months! Your auto and house insurance premiums are priced based on precise, mathematical probabilities. And in your Forex trading business, you can take positions where the mathematical probability is 70%, 80%, 90%, and I've seen cases of 95% for your success!

Go ahead and ask your banker or stock expert the probability of your savings or investment success. You'll get a blank stare! What's the probability your common shares will jump in price tomorrow, next month, or next year? Nobody knows (no matter the degree of expertise they try to sell you on)! Hmmm...does that 75-95% group of Forex losers know that definite mathematical odds in currency prices are available to study before they naively threw their money away?

Suppose for example you were considering the special profit opportunity developing in the New Zealand Dollar last January of 2009. You were considering buying a single mini lot and wondered what the odds were. You would merely use the back-testing feature of the **Track n' Trade Live Forex** platform...

(See Next Page...)

Long term charts, graphs, and data such as you see on this page and throughout this Program are available from http://www.thebestbusinessonearth.com/. However, if you join my TradeMentor.com trading club you'll get a special "*deal*" as my student.

Here you see Forex prices going back to 1995 for the USD/CHF. In this pair the USD is the base currency. One of the most powerful ways to increase your odds is to (1) calculate the average price looking 12 months back and (2) look at a chart with just the closing price and (3) buy or sell when the market line "*crosses*" the 12 month moving average line.

With a touch of the button the chart above turns into this:

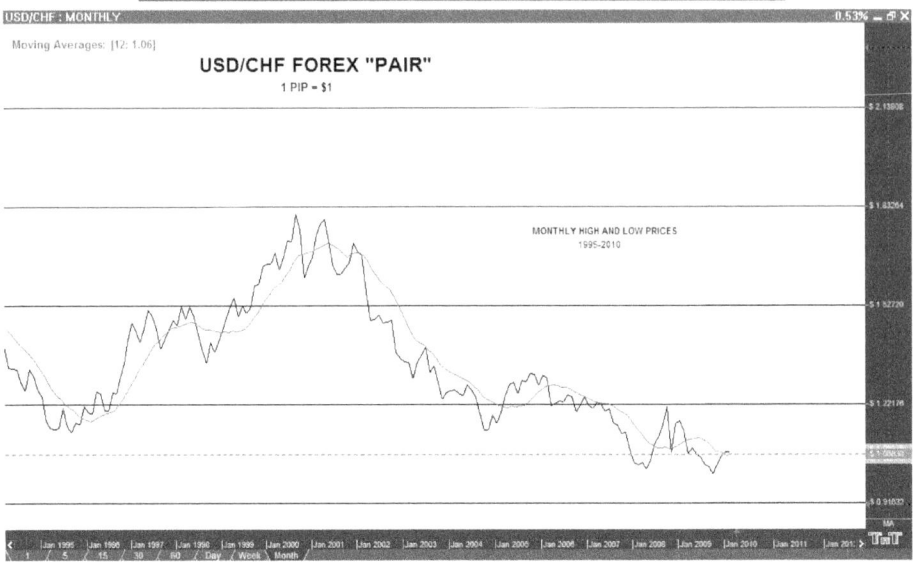

Look at the chart from 2001 onwards where I point out the buying and selling opportunities in this most simple moving average crossover idea:

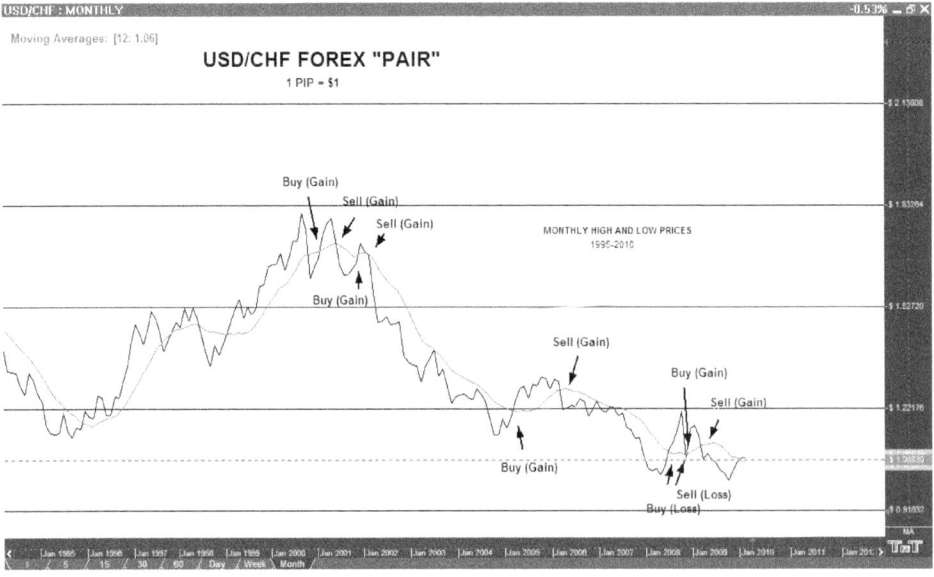

From 2001 to 2010 with this one simple profit opportunity spotting idea you'd have had 8 out of 10 profitable trades — 80%!

The 12 month moving average is just another tool to improve your business operation and planning. I wonder if the 75-95% losers' brokers ever told them about **slow moving average** odds?

How many Forex traders are there in the world? Hundreds of thousands. Therefore there are hundreds of thousands of investment systems and methods. There are millions of drivers but no two steer an automobile the same. Some are very careful and won't ever have an accident. Successful drivers are a small group using the very same roads, driving under the very same road conditions, with the same cars, still they are more successful — why? If you surveyed them, they would say something like, "***Hmmm...I simply follow the rules I learned when I was taught to drive by a competent teacher.***"

They have a sound plan.

You profits will never be guaranteed in Forex, any more than any driver has a guarantee of never having a wreck, but you can study, learn, master your skills — and just like steering a car, you can even get insurance in Forex investing! Both car and Forex insurance policies cost a premium, but they can **guarantee** you won't suffer greater financial loss than you've planned for.

A car can be driven in only one way: you have to step into the driver's seat and drive! Sure, you have to study the driving manuals, and should train in simulators, but you'll never get a driver's license until you hop into the driver's seat and drive. In Forex trading, you can actually run a **complete**, totally realistic, fully-operational Forex business in electronic simulation on your home computer — before you ever place a live order. Try doing that with a McDonald's franchise or **any other** business.

In addition to what you've already learned so far, I will familiarize you with the use of VERY SPECIAL TOOLS in your Forex trading. These three Fundamentals will put you in that envied 5-25% group of successful Forex traders. I am not saying you won't have losses — you absolutely will lose on occasion, just as with all successful business experiences. But you'll never face another opportunity like this to master your destiny and enjoy all the potentials and profits you can. You will have to study, practice and build skill, yet not nearly so much as you may fear. Successful trading is not as easy as "*one, two, three,*" yet there's no business that comes as close to HOW TO MASTER FOREX TRADING!

You can chart anything; time versus movement, illustrated. All statistics; populations, your income, your age, temperature, crime waves, etcetera. In Forex, you create price graphs by charting fluctuations over periods of time. Through this technique, you can see opportunities and dangers that wouldn't be visible by simply looking at a list of numbers.

This is a graph of the cash price for the New Zealand Dollar against the US Dollar. New Zealand has a high standard of living and is part of the 1st world of developed nations. This gives its currency stability and strength backed by sound economics and politics. The price reached a year low on February 7th of 2010.

PRICES CAN ONLY MOVE UP, DOWN, OR SIDEWAYS.

That's all! They can't move backwards, stop, or go in two directions at once. Only UP, DOWN, or SIDEWAYS.

KEY: PRICES TEND TO MOVE IN PARTICULAR PATTERNS.   One of the simplest patterns to identify and begin a business on is the SIMPLE LONG-TERM TREND LINE.   This, the simplest of all chart patterns, is probably the most powerful and consistent business-builder to be found in all the world of Forex. A hermit with access to an internet connected computer can learn to successfully build a monumental business based on a SIMPLE LONG-TERM TREND LINE PATTERN.

When you spot a simple trend on any chart (not just Forex prices!), you can apply a fundamental:

WHEN A "BREAK" FROM A SIMPLE LONG-TERM TREND OCCURS, THE CHART WILL TEND TO MOVE IN THAT DIRECTION.

This is a Law of Nature: That which is in motion tends to continue in motion in the same direction — this is "*momentum*" or "*impetus*" and there's innumerous everyday examples of this law, but let's one in particular:

(See next page…)

105

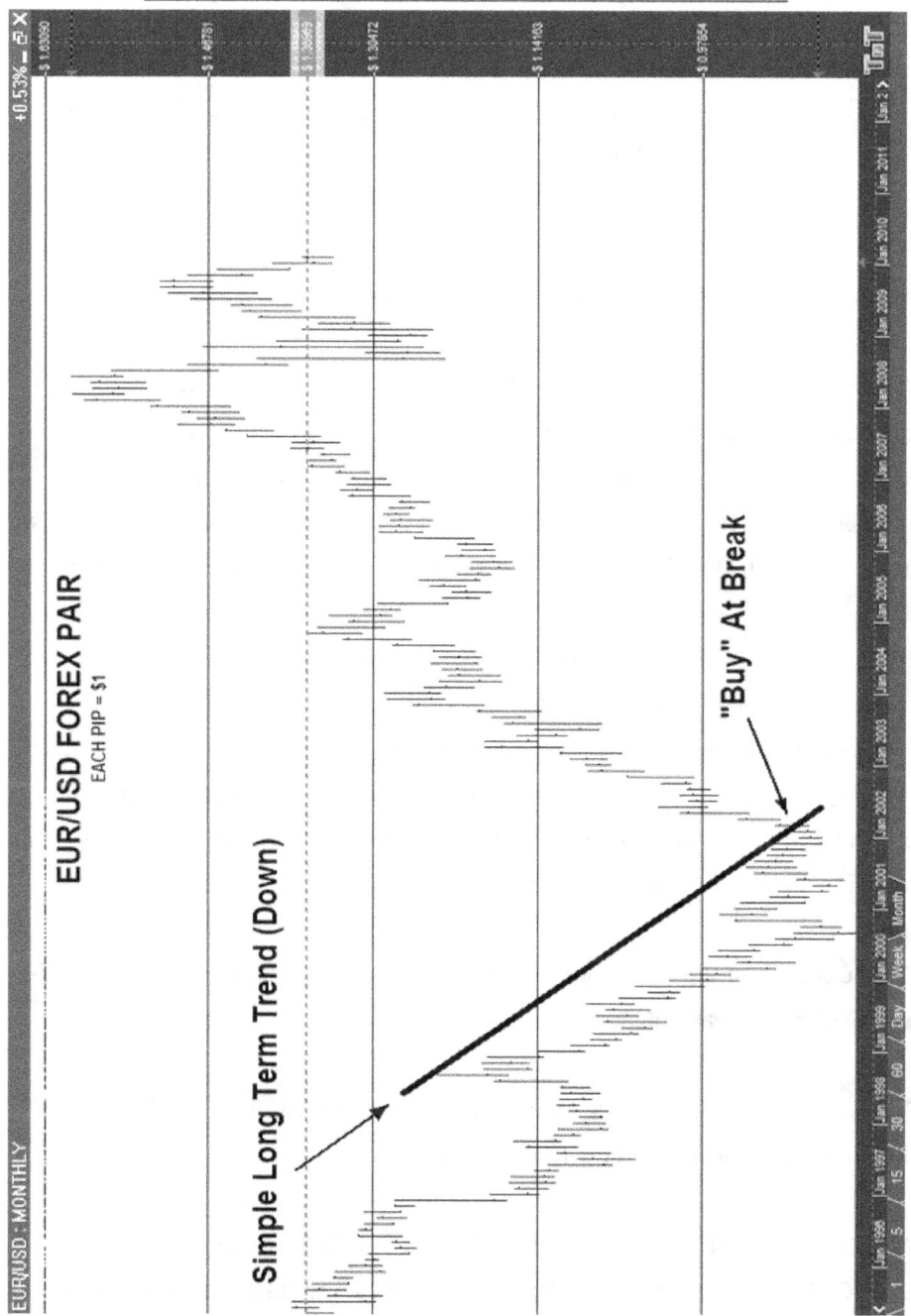

For three years the Euro weakened against the U.S. Dollar. Then it stalled out and moved sideways. Finally it broke up through the simple long-term trend line

$0.8893/€. Think of that price line as a garden snake traveling along a city street looking for a drain to get out of sight (and out of danger from HUMANS!). It has to keep pushing up against the curb till it breaks out to safety. When the price breaks the trend, **as it surely will**, sooner or later, IT WILL TEND TO STAY IN THAT DIRECTION.

Precisely that occurred in the EUR/USD pair in March of 2002.

You could have waited for the break to actually occur before hitting the **BUY** (go long, anticipate increasing strength in the EUR) button in your Track n' Trade Live Forex platform **or**, you could have placed an *"open order"* on the platform instructing the software to buy a EUR/USD mini-lot for you if, BUT ONLY IF, prices broke above $0.9000/€ to be REALLY sure the simple long-term trend was broken.

For example, in February of 2002 how would you have known that prices would break the trend line the next month? You couldn't! You could use your other business tools to get a good idea, but nobody would ever know for certain until it really happened. No problem: you could have placed an open order with your broker to go long (upward), a little above the line itself to be reasonably sure there really is a break — $0.9000/€ for instance.

OR you could just sit, check your computer screen once a day for about 5 minutes, watch, plan, and wait (I'll get to that later).

For the next two years a single mini lot risking just $200 profited $4,133. And all this without duplicating (using internal financing) mini lots.

WITHOUT KNOWING A THING ABOUT INTERNATIONAL FINANCE AND ECONOMICS, you could have built a $1 million-plus business! *"But that's too easy,"* you're saying, *"The EUR could have as easily dropped at any point along the way!"* Of course it could! Remember, in March of 2002, NOBODY KNEW OR COULD HAVE KNOWN, WHAT THE EURO PRICE WOULD DO! But you **don't have to know** in order to build a sound profitable business in the Euro with none of the multitude of problems associated with, and inherent in, **All** other businesses. Here's how to add prudence to you business plan in the EUR/USD:

THE STOP-LOSS

Comforting isn't it! Indeed it is...

Imagine you're hitchhiking from the southern part of Forexico to the northern tip of this fictional country. Traffic laws don't exist in Forexico — people drive in any which way they want on this country's highways. If your wife is attractive drug-lord bandits will stop you, rob you, and **VIOLATE** your wife. When you drive at night you look AT an oncoming car's headlights to see if there's the silhouette of a loaded burro or broken down car driving without lights on the road.

That's **IF** you drive in Forexico.

But you're smarter than that so you leave your attractive wife at home along with your expensive car, fine clothes, and fat wallet. And you do Forexico on foot. You have no way of knowing where each car is headed, so your wisest choice would be to HITCH A RIDE ON A NORTHBOUND VEHICLE. It may continue northward for awhile and perhaps begin to veer easterly, or to the west. You'd perk up then and become keenly aware of this car's changing directions. If the car suddenly headed south, you'd get out and wait for another northern bound car to pick you up. You may zig-zag across Forexico, but you're **sure** to reach your destination using this method!

The Forex markets are lot like Forexico; prices don't travel in nice, neat straight, uni-directional lines! Your goal is to stay with that dynamic, travelling line AS LONG AS IT CONTINUES TO MOVE IN YOUR FAVOR. If it should turn in the opposite direction from which you're profiting, GET OFF!

Placing **pre-planned** stop-loss orders with the TnT Live Forex platform is the best way to insure this. **Pre-planning** is vital to your success. You have about the same chances for winning a jackpot in Las Vegas in a poorly planned business. Yes, some people do hit jackpots, but it's nothing more than luck and gambling. How many of the 75-95% Forex losers do you think have a plan? You know the answer to that (I trust you're now **at least starting** to respect this, HOW TO MASTER FOREX TRADING!).

Let's go back to March of 2002: you were watching EUR/USD prices "*wiggle*" up towards $0.9000/€, knowing full well that the "*wiggling*" would break the simple long-term downtrend to the upside. You begin your business plan **now**, **before** the break. This is called PRIOR PLANNING and it's at the heart of every successful business operation. You've decided to buy one EUR/USD mini lot if the price ever moves to $0.9000/€. You've prudently opened your account at the special brokerage I use exclusively and deposited margin money well before you ever made a trade by clicking on the button on the start-up page of TnT Live Forex that says: "*Open A Fx Real Money Account*" after downloading the special deal I have arranged for you at http://www.thebestbusinessonearth.com/

This is the wise thing to do; you can't buy a Forex lot unless the margin account is set-up. It will sit there until you decide (nobody from the special Forex software trading platform or brokerage I use will call you to talk you into anything!) to buy or sell. Some brokerages now pay interest on your margin money and you may even deposit a Treasury bill (T-Bill) as margin money if you like. With an established margin account, back in March of 2002, you could have given the TnT Live Forex automated trading platform these instructions: "IF THE PRICE OF THE EUR/USD FOREX "PAIR" EVER HITS $0.9000/€ BUY ONE MINI LOT FOR MY ACCOUNT."

But that's not all you can do: at the **same time** you can establish a stop-loss plan, as well!

Experience and study will give you the best placement of stop-loss orders: there are advanced strategies that will increase your profits — and it won't cost you any college tuition to learn it. I can tell you that Forex traders who are afraid to lose set them too tight. And traders who are overconfident of their ability set them too loose. The March price of the EUR/USD did, in fact, hit $0.9000/€ and your automatic trading helper (TnT Forex Live) would have automatically bought a Forex lot for you at the **MARKET PRICE** that prevailed **as soon as possible after the $0.9000/€ price level had been hit**.

That is, when the price actually hit $0.9000/€, your pre-existing order ("*open order*") went live.

At that moment, your order to buy one EUR/USD pair went into the electronic auction, BUT THE ELECTRONIC EXCHANGE DIDN'T SUDDENLY STOP JUST BECAUSE YOUR ORDER WAS HIT. Business went on as usual, so the actual price at which your "*order*" was "*filled*" may not be exactly $0.9000/€. It may be lower (which would give you more profit than a "*fill*" at exactly $0.9000/€ would have, and a lower fill would be just fine. Why! Because you not only fulfilled your objective "*to get on board only if the market was going the way you wanted to go*" but you also got in at a more profitable price.

By pre-selecting a price above the trend line ($0.9000/€) the price would **have** to move the way you want it to (up) or your order would never be filled. That's the **only way** to ever enter **any** market — only when the price actually moves the way you want it to. The 75-95% losers just jumped into **any** passing car in Forexico **hoping** it would take them where they wanted to go! But hoping is worse than flipping a coin. You cannot run a business on hope. And it certainly doesn't take a Ph.D. in finance (like mine) to employ a stop-loss — the most basic strategy to your plan.

Once the EUR/USD price triggered your $0.9000/€ open "*limit*" order, you became a passenger on the "*Euro line express.*" You intend to take a ride on the "*Euro line*

111

express" as long as it moves in your direction; in this case, **UP**. If it should turn downward, when do you want **OFF** the "*Euro line express?*" Ideally, you place your stop-loss order far enough below (when **buying** a contract) your entry point so that it will never be reached when you're right, but close enough below your entry point to stop your losses to as little as possible when you're wrong. "*Now that's like carefully planning all the places to see on a vacation to an exact budget, not too cheap but not too expensive!*" NOBODY CAN TELL THE FUTURE, hence you must be as **prudent and wise** as possible in planning the stop-loss order.

Let's analyze this: EUR/USD prices snaked along a near perfect down-line for several years. It would be prudent then to set the stop-loss point **just below the bottom of the extension of the near perfect-down line**, or below $0.8856/€. Let's set it at $0.8800/€. You entered when the price hit $0.9000/€, but let's say prices then began to drop. Down, down, down they went and finally hit $0.8800/€. Your stop-loss order was triggered and your one EUR/USD mini-lot **sold** at about $0.8800/€ (remember trading didn't stop to wait for you on the electronic cash Forex exchange). Each PIP move is $1, so you would have lost a total of $200 ($0.9000/€ - $0.8800/€ equals $0.0200/€ or 200 PIPs).

So setting a stop-loss at $0.8800/€ may have been prudent, even though $200 may seem like a lot to lose you could have lost much, much more.

But in reality this would have been a stellar trade. The market never fell back to trigger your stop-loss. As prices move in your favor on a profitable trade, keep raising that stop-loss point to either stop your losses further, or to "**lock in**" any profits you've already earned. For instance, on March 4th the market hit $0.9000/€. One week later (about March 12) the EUR/USD was above $0.9200/€… for a $200 profit (100% in a **week!**) You could have then moved your stop-loss up to $0.9000/€ — the break even point (less the spread you pay to the special Forex brokerage I use exclusively).

Just after May 1st prices shot up to $0.9905/€. You may have moved your stop up to $0.9705/€ to lock in a $705 ($0.9705/€ - $0.9000/€ equals $0.0705/€) profit.

In June the market hit a high of $1.0226/€ and you would have "trailed" your stop to $1.0026/€. In July the market would have retraced hitting your stop and taking you out of the market with a $1,026 profit ($1.0026/€ - $0.9000/€ equals $0.1026/€ or 1,026 PIPs). You can see what EUR/USD prices did — that climbed all the way to $1.2994/€ so trailing your stops too close would have cost you **potential** profits. The more profits you accumulate, the farther behind you can afford to place your stops.

The sharpness of the trending down or up-line will help you determine accurate initial stop points, **but experience alone** is the only "*mentor*" to turn to for advice in placing stops. HOW TO MASTER FOREX TRADING is a complete program, specifically designed to afford you plenty of experience before you invest your money in your Forex business.

CREATING PYRAMIDS

"Pyramids" Like the word "*Forex,*" sound negative to most folks. But do you want to be like "*most people*" living in quiet desperation. "*Most people*" (55% according to a 2010 national survey) are frustrated in their uninteresting jobs, unhappy that their incomes have not kept up with inflation, and keep less and less of their money due to the soaring cost of health insurance, and, therefore, are going to end up dead broke and unfulfilled by age 65 (social security statistics) and of little value to themselves and the rest of society!

See... http://www.cbsnews.com/stories/2010/01/05/national/main6056611.shtml

I'm not being mean; in truth dissatisfied workers don't spread joy...they spread misery and like it or not we're all swimming in the same pool.

The normal reaction to the word "*pyramid*" is, "*pyramids are illegal.*" Pyramid chain letters where you send $1 to the person you receive the letter from are postal crime! It only became public knowledge in the 90s that the Social Security System (that I mentioned above) is a pyramid scheme instigated by Congress! And like all chain letters it's running out of money as I'm sure you well know! The Social In-Security System has become a national joke.

Pyramids are elegant, parsimonious, awe inspiring business structures. The officer of every corporation hopes someday to be in a position to **pyramid** his company as President and Chairman of the Board reaping an average salary of $9.25 million in 2009. And you can easily be at the top of your very own business pyramid through the Forex market!

Take a U.S. dollar bill out of your wallet. Turn it over and what do you see? A pyramid. Wow! Why is there a pyramid on a buck? Congress approved the use of a pyramid on our currency (the strongest in the world) on June 20, 1782 because it symbolizes STRENGTH and ENDURANCE. The pyramid's unfinished apex symbolizes entrepreneurship in that there's always more work to be done in building a great country. The "*All-seeing Eye of God*" on top of the pyramid emphasizes the importance of putting spiritual work (such as forgiveness) above material endeavors.

The Founding Fathers wanted emphasize that strength is rooted in God, and that progress must be under His watchful eye. The words "ANNUIT COEPTIS" encircling the top of the seal means "**HE APPROVES OUR UNDERTAKINGS**." The Latin words under the pyramid, "**NOVUS ORDO SECLORUM**," means a "*New Order of the Ages*," signifying the freedom of the People to **self**-govern (there's that word "*self*" again). The Roman Numerals at the base of the pyramidal centerpiece are a reminder of our Nation's birth date — 1776.

HOW TO MASTER FOREX TRADING teaches you to build pyramids with pre-set stops, giving you the occasion to build greater wealth than you've ever heard of!

115

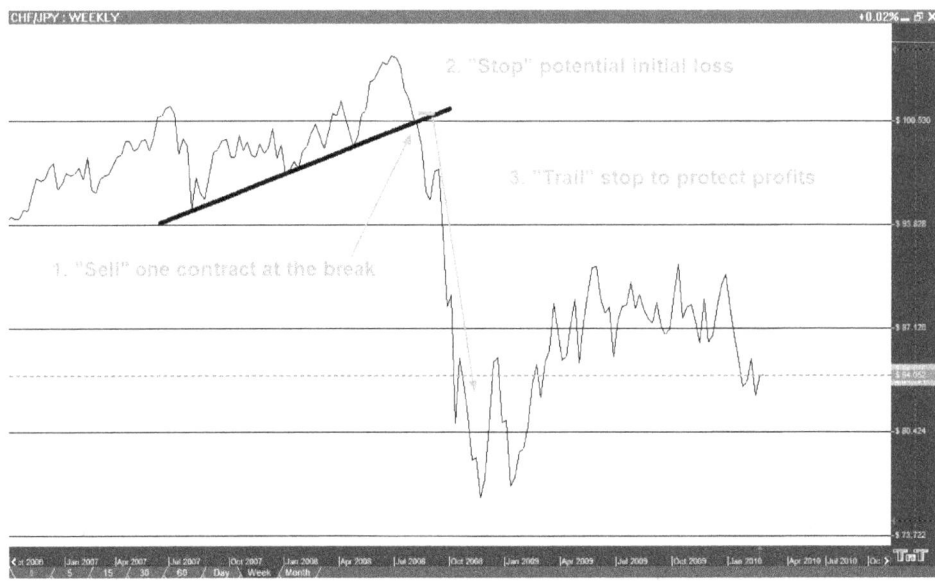

YOU DON'T CARE IF PRICES GO UP **OR** DOWN IN FOREX!

The United States is NOT the only important country in the world. Two other important countries are Switzerland and Japan. These two strong 1st world currencies trade as the CHF/JPY "*FOREX*" PAIR. This is called a "*cross*" pair because it does not involve the U.S. dollar directly (with the foreign currency as the base) or indirectly (with the U.S. Dollar as the base currency). This trade lasting just over 2 months (76 days) in the CHF/JPY in 2008 yielded $2,741.70 on $200 invested. How could you have built a pyramid around the CHF/JPY business of 08'? Suppose you did just one-tenth as well?

Some months ago you noticed CHF/JPY prices snaking along a near perfect up-trend line pattern on the weekly chart, notice how cross rates charting a **rise** in one foreign currency base pair (in this case the Swiss Franc a.k.a. "*Swissy*") means it's strengthening against some other foreign currency (in this case the Japanese yen a.k.a. "*yen*").

116

Confusing?

Have you ever tried to read a **Wall Street Journal**? The first time you try to read one, you'll be stumped — it all looks like Chinese! But read it awhile and suddenly it will all make perfect sense to you! I threw you a curve ball with this cross-rate chart where 1 PIP does NOT equal $1 (don't worry the TnT Live Forex platform automatically calculates this for you), but you'll be zipping through all the charts before you know it! The reason the CHF/JPY chart does not have 1 PIP equal to $1 is that your profit or loss is denominated into two foreign currencies. Your U.S. Dollar profit or loss (which is all you **REALLY** care about) has to be converted in and converted out of the trade. This used to be a real hassle by hand but the TnT Live Forex platform will do that for you automatically!

Euros, Pounds, Yens, Dollars (U.S. Canadian, Australian, or New Zealand), it doesn't matter. We have happened to have spotted a perfect uptrend "*snaking*" along in MEXICAN PESO prices on this **monthly chart (**which gives us a different perspective from looking at a **daily chart**). You would have known something was going to happen with prices here by **simply watching the perfect up-trend line**; you wouldn't even have had to read all the internet headlines or watch the evening news:

MEXICO ON BRINK OF COLLAPSE (AGAIN)!

The daily chart is…

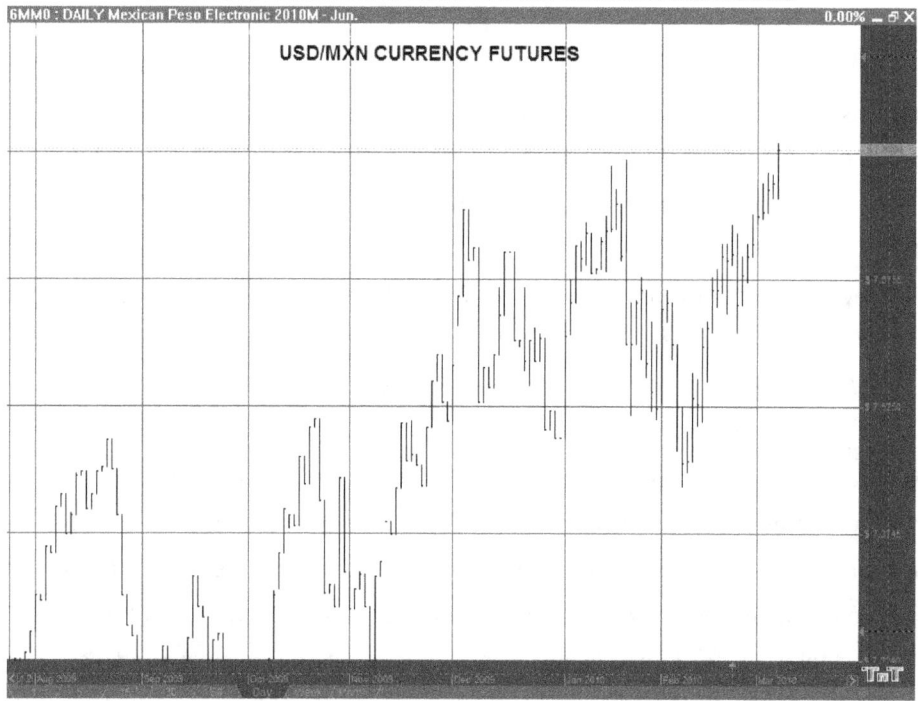

Quite a different view!

Mexican pesos would, sooner or later break the up-trend, so you could have prepared yourself for a profit opportunity by watching the MONTHLY instead of the daily chart….

You would have sold a single mini lot if the price hit MXN 8.5991/$. Remember that the golden rule is always **buy low and sell high**. To buy a mini lot of any currency, whether in the Forex market or contract in the commodity futures market, means that *"you're buying low and selling high;"* that is, you **buy** an item at today's price, expecting to sell it to someone else at a higher price in the future. To **sell** a mini lot or a contract, whether in the Forex market or commodity futures market, means you contract to sell that mini lot (or contract) sometime in the future **based on today's price**.

I can acquire a car, for example that you want.

It's worth $20,000 today, but I happen to believe it will cost only $10,000 three months from now (for whatever reasons), so I'll **sell** the car to you at **today's** price of $20,000 and agree to deliver it in three months (for example). Before delivery time comes. I buy and make a tidy $10,000 profit.

But now I scared you, didn't I, you're thinking, *"There's the catch! If I made a wrong move in this currency business, some armored truck is going to back up and dump a pile of Mexican Pesos on my lawn! I knew there was a catch to all this!"*

No, that's one of the major benefits of the Forex market: LIQUIDITY, the total number of traders, as my nephew Zach would say is, *"Humongous — it's totally awesome!"* The sheer vastness of the crowd of traders makes it easy to buy and sell your mini lots. Incidentally, I showed you the Mexican Peso currency futures contract for a reason. Mexico's government has so severely mismanaged it's country and economy that nobody trusts their currency. Nobody wants to trade it. That's why you WON'T find the USD/MXN symbol in the TnT Forex Live platform.

The futures market has it's benefits (like insurance in the form of options and the **Commitment of Traders** indicator) but there are a lot of illiquid mini lots over there you can't trade; lumber, Mexican pesos, ethanol, rice and oats!

By sticking to the most popular pairs in Forex (called the MAJORS) you know you've got the most liquidity:

PAIR	CURRENCIES (NICKNAME)
EUR/USD	**Euro / US Dollar (Fiber)**
USD/JPY	US Dollar / Japanese Yen (Gopher)
GBP/USD	UK Sterling / US Dollar (Cable)
USD/CHF	US Dollar / Swiss Franc (Swizzy)
USD/CAD	US Dollar / Canadian Dollar (Loonie)
AUD/USD	Australian Dollar / US Dollar (Aussie)
NZD/USD	New Zealand Dollar / US Dollar (Kiwi)

Some currency pairs are more volatile than others. This makes them better to use in trades as they trend. The best currencies to trade are those of countries that are the major role players in the world economy (these are called *"G7"* countries). The G7 was formed in 1976, when Canada joined the Group of Six: France, Germany, Italy, Japan, the United Kingdom, and the United States.

You'll see that the spread on the *"major pairs"* from the G7s is much lower than on less popular pairs from weak countries with chronic economic and political instability. **Example:** The spread on the EUR/USD is between 1.5 and 3 pips because the major countries making up the Euro Currency and the United States are BOTH G7 countries.

Take South Africa for instance. I think Nelson Mandela is a pretty cool guy. His story is a classic *"Think and Grow Rich"* example of a definite major purpose and definite desire having transmuted his dream to reality. But I DON'T trust the WACKO government that has evolved from the hatred not only of whites against blacks (apartheid) but also of blacks against whites. Change happened WAY TOO FAST IN SOUTH AFRICA and because of that it is now an unstable 3rd world political economy. The law of an equal or greater benefit will come of the political economic tragedy that is South Africa but it will be in the future as I write this.

Because of this the spread on the USD/ZAR pair is about 60 pips — 20 times more expensive to trade than the EUR/USD — reflecting the high instability of this African political economy.

The safest place to learn Forex trading is in the EUR/USD pair where a full 1/3 of all Forex trades occur. Then, after you know what you're doing, you can venture out into other pairs on the list below. For instance, there are some CROSS PAIRS that are also good for trading.

So when we add the two strongest CROSSES and delete the two weakest MAJORS from your list of TRADABLES above here's an alternative group to trade:

PAIR	CURRENCIES (NICKNAME)
EUR/USD	Euro / US Dollar (Fiber)
USD/JPY	US Dollar / Japanese Yen (Gopher)
GBP/USD	UK Sterling / US Dollar (Cable)
USD/CHF	US Dollar / Swiss Franc (Swizzy)
USD/CAD	US Dollar / Canadian Dollar (Loonie)
GBP/JPY	Euro/Yen Cross (Geppy)
EUR/GBP	Euro/Cable Cross (Chunnel)

THE TRADABLE EIGHTEEN

There are many official currencies that are used all over the world, but there only a handful of currencies that are traded actively in the Forex market. In currency trading, only the most economically and politically stable countries have currencies that are traded enough to be liquid. For example, due to the size and strength of the United States economy, the American dollar is the world's most actively traded currency.

The eight most traded currencies are the U.S. dollar (USD), the euro (EUR), the British pound (GBP), the Japanese yen (JPY), the Swiss franc (CHF), the Canadian dollar (CAD), the Australian dollar (AUD), and finally the New Zealand dollar (NZD)

As you've learned, your currency business is traded in pairs. Mathematically, there are 27 different currency pairs that can be arranged from the eight currencies above. Of these 27 however, there are only 18 currency pairs that are conventionally quoted by Forex market makers as safely tradable due to their overall liquidity.

These pairs are:

PAIR	CURRENCIES (NICKNAME)
EUR/USD	Euro / US Dollar (Fiber)
USD/JPY	US Dollar / Japanese Yen (Gopher)
GBP/USD	UK Sterling / US Dollar (Cable)
USD/CHF	US Dollar / Swiss Franc (Swizzy)
USD/CAD	US Dollar / Canadian Dollar (Loonie)
AUD/USD	Australian Dollar / US Dollar (Aussie)
NZD/USD	New Zealand Dollar / US Dollar (Kiwi)
GBP/JPY	Euro/Yen Cross (Geppy)
EUR/GBP	Euro/Cable Cross (Chunnel)
EUR/JPY	Euro / Japanese Yen Cross
CHF/JPY	Swiss Franc / Japanese Yen Cross
GBP/CHF	UK Sterling / Swiss Franc Cross
EUR/CHF	Euro / Swiss Franc Cross
EUR/CAD	Euro / Canadian Dollar Cross
EUR/AUD	Euro / Australian Dollar Cross
AUD/JPY	Australian Dollar / Japanese Yen Cross
AUD/CAD	Australian Dollar / Canadian Dollar Cross
AUD/NZD	Australian Dollar / New Zealand Dollar Cross

The total amount of currency trading involving these 18 pairs represents 99% of ALL trading volume in the FX market. Another reason this is How to Master Forex Trading is that this manageable number of business choices makes trading a lot less complicated compared to dealing with stocks; which has thousands of bewildering choices.

No matter how experienced you become as a Forex trader you will almost certainly never trade outside of the list above!

In March of 2009 a retired Superior Court Judge attended one of my stock investing lectures at the Investment U Annual Conference in St. Petersburg, Florida. Several days later he called me at my office and began talking commodities (my second favorite topic!). He'd lost thousands of dollars just the way I described earlier in this program, and wasn't exactly enthusiastic about the subject.

When I explained the difference between **dabbling in the market** and running your own **business** in an even better business than commodities, Forex, he realized it all made sense.

I briefly described the simple trend following system and gave him a few examples, such as you've seen here, to study. I then pointed out how the how the Aussie / Loonie Cross Pair had just broken a perfect two month downtrend. He nodded, said it sounded interesting, and departed.

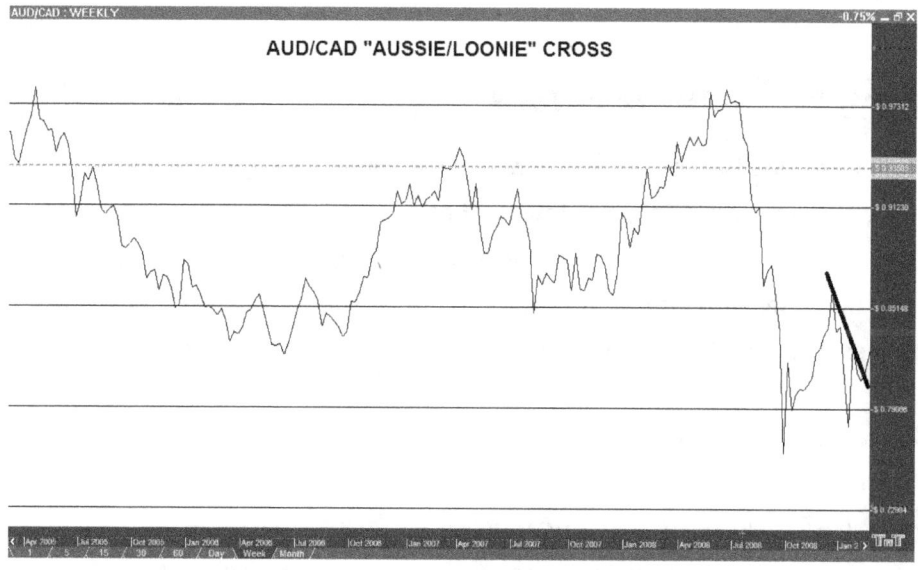

The judge phoned me in late November (just eight months after our conversation). Not expecting that he had taken action on the materials I had given him, I casually asked, *"Did you know that the Aussie / Loonie Cross kept rising out of its trend break I showed you?"* *"I know!,"* he said, *"That was the easiest $15,000 I ever made!"*

Here's what the judge did...

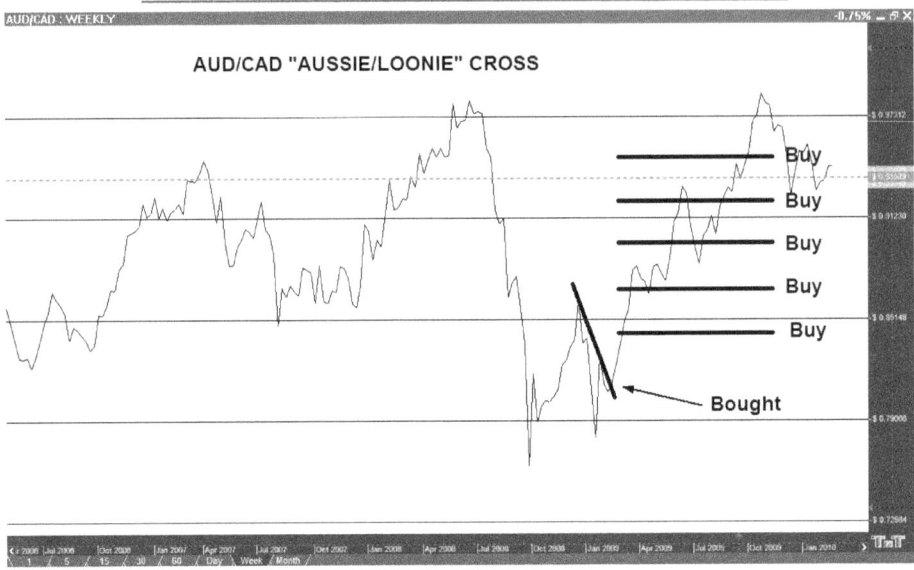

The judge waited for the break to continue then pull back slightly on the daily chart. He then "*scaled up*" (used **internal financing** to purchase new lots). His plan was to scale up at each 250 PIP level. He "*trailed*" his stop-losses (kept moving them up, closer and closer, as his profits accumulated). His Aussie / Loonie Cross business finally ended at his pre-set stop-loss point of AUD0.9828/CAD.

Here's what happened…

1 mini lot, bought at 0.8132 AUD/CAD, $200 margin (out of pocket)

1 mini lot, bought at 0.8347 AUD/CAD, —0— margin (internal financing)

2 mini lots, bought at 0.8699 AUD/CAD, —0— margin   "

4 mini lots, bought at 0.9225 AUD/CAD, —0— margin   "

8 mini lots, bought at 0.9483 AUD/CAD, —0— margin   "

16 mini lots, bought at 0.9733 AUD/CAD, —0— margin   "

When stopped-out at AUD 0.9828/CAD, here's what his lots had generated:

1   Mini Lot @ 0.8132 AUD/CAD = $250

1   Mini lot @ 0.8347 AUD/CAD = $500

126

2	Mini lots @ 0.8699 AUD/CAD = $1,000
4	Mini lots @ 0.9225 AUD/CAD = $2,000
8	Mini lots @ 0.9483 AUD/CAD = $4,000
16	Mini lots @ 0.9733 AUD/CAD = $8,000

Total profits = $15,250 (less the 8 pip spread/ per mini lot for the electronic brokerage fee, x 32 mini lots = $220.16) for a **net profit of $15,029.84**. Initial out of pocket investment was $200 which equals a 7,514.92$ return on investment in approximately 34 weeks. That's over 11,000% annually!

■■■■■■

I had met another man at that same conference in March of 2009, who hated the commodity market! He had lost over $180,000 with a commodity broker and **couldn't explain how it happened!** I remember he was **very** cynical, but I managed to explain the simple, sound, "*trend-line*" fact. He became more and more interested when I explained how you can start with much less money in Forex and never lose more than you put in. I showed him the trend break in the Aussie/Loonie cross-pair.

He said, "*Well, I'm going on a Amazon trip (he's a marine biologist) until the end of May, so I hope the market hasn't risen too much before then!*" I then explained that he could **pre-place** instructions in his electronic platform that automatically trades the special electronic brokerage account on autopilot in his absence (both of which I use at http://www.thebestbusinessonearth.com/), so that, **whatever happened**, he would be "*covered.*"

He opened a $1,000 margin account (again through http://www.thebestbusinessonearth.com/) and placed these instructions in his TnT Live Forex platform with the **AUTOPILOT PLUG-IN**:

127

"BUY ONE AUD/CAD MINI LOT IF THE PRICE EVER REACHES 0.8132 AUD/CAD AND, IF THAT HAPPENS ESTABLISH AS STOP LOSS AT 0.7907AUD/CAD. IF THE PRICE RISES TRAIL THE STOP LOSS TO LOCK IN GAINS. IF THE PRICE REACHES 0.8347 AUD/CAD BUY ANOTHER CONTRACT. IF PRICES CONTINUE TO ADVANCE TRAIL A STOP LOSS 225 PIPS BEHIND CURRENT PRICES."

When he returned from the Amazon at the end of May, 2009, his AUD/CAD currency business had just been terminated when his **two mini lots** (he only wanted to scale up once) were closed (sold) at 0.9091 AUD/CAD. Here's his accounting

1 mini lot bought at 0.8132 AUD/CAD and sold at 0.9093 AUD/CAD =
     $899.19 profit.
1 mini lot bought at 0.8347 AUD/CAD and sold at 0.9093 AUD/CAD =
     $610.13 profit.

TOTAL PROFIT
     $1,509.32
     (Spread charge, @ $6.88/mini lot)
          - $13.76

NET PROFIT
     $1,495.56

He said he couldn't have checked the internet to save his life, yet this man's $200 returned $1,495.56 in just about 4 months, or **over 2,000% annualized!**

Both these men acted on the **very same event**; one turned it into over $15,000 profit, and the other, over $1,000 profit. What's the difference? PERCEPTION!

I'd like you to read the number of times the letter "*F*" appears in the passage below.

FUNCTIONAL FAMILIES ARE THE RESULT OF YEARS OF STABLE PARENTING BY HIGH INTEGRITY HEADS OF HOUSEHOLDS AS SHOWN THROUGH SCIENTIFIC STUDY.

Did you find 3 Fs? That's common. There's actually 6 Fs. This is a trick of perception since most people sound out words as they read in their mind where the Fs for instance in the word *"of"* sound out as Vs (*"of"* is phonetically pronounced *"ov"*). The Fs were there all the time but your perception blocked half of them. This also happens in other areas of your life…

> "I've got the deal of the century for you! A close friend brought me a license to own a new franchise that will likely explode upward in value and make you and I wealthier than we've ever dreamed! Here's how it works: *I can option the license for $100,000 but I've only got $90,000 in cash. You finance the other $10,000, and I'll give you a full partnership — We'll be 50:50 partners even though you only forked out 10%.*
>
> *Here's what you'll own: The license is for a retail store that'll sell just about everything under the sun, liquor, groceries, and deli food, with an ingenious twist! You and I'll sell everything for up to forty percent more than stores in the area will be peddling. Ingenuous, right?!"*
>
> "Huh? You're not interested in this fantastic opportunity? How come? By the way the name of our franchise will be 7-eleven!"

When I pose this situation to my MBA students, only one or two of them out of every hundred accepted my offer before they knew it was 7-eleven. This example isn't intended to represent the world, but pay attention to these statistics. Just 5% of Americans are the doers in the world, the rest are watching TV, playing on the computer, and saying, *"If only I'd' a' done this or that…"* When it comes to seminars the numbers are worse; just 1 to 2% of all those who attend Real Estate seminars ever do anything with what they learned.

HOW TO MASTER FOREX TRADING is my personal manifesto. I'm writing this to change your world — if just for the few **doers** who act on what I am teaching here.

You're surrounded right now by **countless** opportunities. Before you can strike it rich you have to swing the pick. If you take action on what you've learning here you stand to increase your net worth and income tremendously. This **is** a given! If you put forth the effort, a natural law comes into play: Napoleon Hill calls it COSMIC HABIT FORCE. It's just that simple.

OPPORTUNITYISNOWHERE...

YOU NEVER KNOW WHAT YOU CAN DO TIL YOU TRY!

CURRENCY FUTURES

Before the personal computer and internet was powerful enough to allow you to trade Forex lots the CURRENCY FUTURES CONTRACT was introduced at the Chicago Mercantile Exchange (CME) in 1972, less than one year after the system of fixed exchange rates was abandoned along with the gold standard. Some commodity traders at the CME didn't have access to the INTER-BANK EXCHANGE MARKETS (FOREX FORWARD MARKET) in the early 1970s, when they believed that significant changes were about to take place in the currency market.

Currency futures gave them access.

There are two fabulous things about currency futures that help you with Forex trading. The first is that insurance is available through these markets in the form of **OPTIONS**. But not all 18 pairs offer it — only the 11 most active.

I'll explain more about options in the chapter on insurance but here's the futures currency contracts traded and those which have currency futures options you can use as insurance …

PAIR	Options
EUR/USD	YES
USD/JPY	YES
GBP/USD	YES
USD/CHF	YES
USD/CAD	YES
AUD/USD	YES
NZD/USD	YES
GBP/JPY	NO
EUR/GBP	YES
EUR/JPY	YES
CHF/JPY	NO
GBP/CHF	YES
EUR/CHF	YES
EUR/CAD	NO
EUR/AUD	NO
AUD/JPY	NO
AUD/CAD	NO
AUD/NZD	NO

The second fabulous fact about currency futures is that they track who's who in these markets. The first player is known as the COMMERCIALS. These are big banks who trade in these markets to protect their clients from losses in their business from interest rate risk. Next are the LARGE SPECULATORS who are hedge funds with millions of dollars at risk in outright speculation.

The last group is the SMALL SPECULATORS who trade smaller amounts of money.

The group that you want to watch is the LARGE SPECULATORS. These **Certified Trading Advisors** are very good at spotting market turns in the major trend. When that happens as they shift as a group from long to short or vice versa. This gives you a powerful clue to help confirm your simple trend following system.

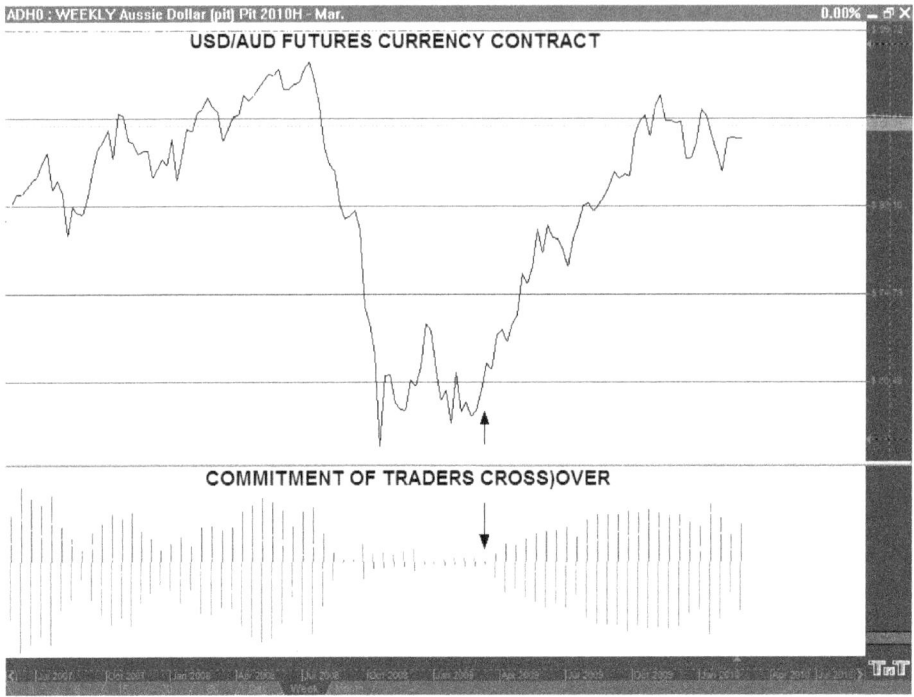

Some students ask me, *"Why don't I just trade the currency futures market?"* The answer lies in the contract size and over-regulated nature of the futures markets. The Australian Dollar contract requires a deposit of $3,375 to control $100,000 worth of currency. If you scale this down to the 10,000 unit mini-Forex lot that means that you have to put MORE money down as a deposit — $337.50 instead of $200!

Plus, you have to trade ten times the mini lot Forex value.

When Ford Model T cars came out in 1914 they had two gears — forward and reverse! Wouldn't that be an awkward way to drive now that we are used to 5 or more gear speeds?! Whenever you can trade smaller increments for the same fractional transaction cost you should do so.

That's why the mini lot makes so much sense!

For instance, you cannot trade the Australian Dollar Futures Contract with $1,000 because you would only have less than a third of the required deposit. But over in the Forex market it's no problem at all since as you grow you can build to trading 10 mini lots for the same total value — $100,000.

So don't ever trade currency futures but do use the additional information these markets provide. You can get the commitment of traders on the Track n' Trade Live Futures platform through http://www.thebestbusinessonearth.com/

Since we're on the topic of futures trading I'll show you how you can expand into this business once you've mastered Forex. First, remember that you shouldn't start here since you can lose more than you put in. Commodities is NOT The a perfect business for this reason…but it can come close if you play your cards properly.

If you saw the movie, TRADING PLACES, you saw how pyramiding is a double edge sword. Let me explain using an example you are likely aware of. You've probably heard the *"outrage"* over all the profits oil traders made when oil prices skyrocketed between 2002 and 2008. The reality is that the Federal Government did NOTHING to protect the public from these advances and **commodity traders deserve every dime they earned**!

In fact you could have earned $113,640 per crude oil futures contract in that run!

I noticed in 2002 that a very special tool gave a signal to buy on the monthly charts. I told my students and only one did anything with this information. I'll explain that tool in another chapter — called the Bulls N' Bears Red Light Green Light System.

The signal said it was time to BUY oil. But other than going down to the gas station and buying it by the quart, how could you have made a profit on this piece of news? By turning to a Crude Oil price chart!

Every 1¢ move in Crude Oil equals a $10 profit or loss in your account (a crude oil contract controls 1,000 barrels; therefore, 1,000/100¢ = $10).

The Margin (deposit) requirement on a crude oil contract is $5,400, so every $5.40 rise in the price of oil would allow you to pyramid and internally finance another contract (earning you another 540¢ X $10/¢= $5,400).

May 1st, 2003, BUY ONE CRUDE OIL CONTRACT @ $25.37
    Out-of-pocket expense = $5,400

August 1st, 2003, BUY ANOTHER CRUDE OIL CONTRACT @ $30.77
    Out-of-pocket expense = $0

April 1st, 2004, BUY TWO CRUDE OIL CONTRACT @ $36.17
    Out-of-pocket expense = $0

You've pyramided your profits, but have built an **inverse pyramid**: as you can see this isn't a very stable structure...

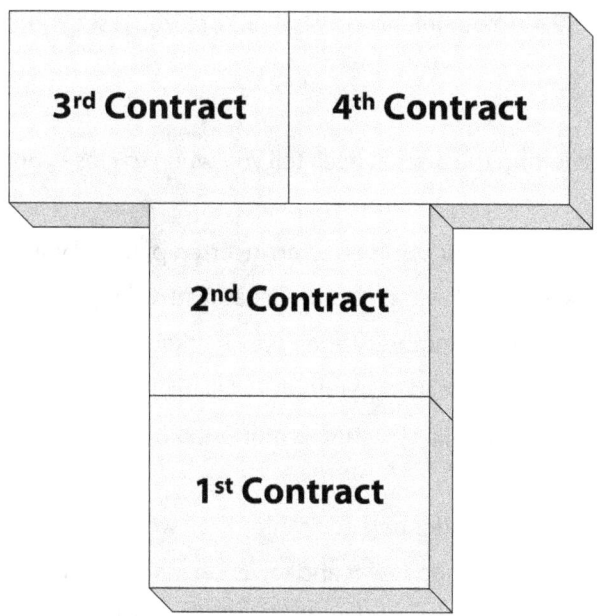

At $37.00, your Crude Oil business looks like this:

First contract bought at $25.37 =$11.63 Gain X $1,000 =
$11,630 Profit

Second contract bought at $30.77 = $6.23 Gain X $1,000 =
$6,230 Profit

Third and fourth lots bought at $36.17 = $0.83 X 1,000 =
$830 Profit

TOTAL PROFITS TO DATE:

$18,690 on a $5,400 investment = 346% in 11 months.

Now Crude Oil prices would, sooner or later, reverse and you'd have provided for this by establishing a liquidation point using a stop loss order NEVER ALLOWING YOU TO LOSE MORE THAN 45% OF YOUR MARGIN. That's $2,430 amounting to a stop-loss trail of $2.43. Your initial entry is $25.37 so you'd set your initial stop-loss at $22.94.

In this way we're letting the market itself tell you when to close your business.

But if you keep growing your business as an inverted pyramid you'll not only make money very quickly but will also go broke just as fast! Going broke is always a distinct possibility in the commodity and Forex markets. For this reason, many traders prefer to PILLAR instead of pyramid: ADDING ONLY ONE NEW CONTRACT AS PROFITS ALLOW. The pillar structure is more stable than an inverted pyramid.

A very successful futures trader named Stanley Kroll would buy a large number of contracts initially and then add fewer and fewer on market reactions — pullbacks. This is also safer than an inverted pyramid but pillaring is the least risky strategy of all.

As a beginner I suggest that you PILLLAR INSTEAD OF PYRAMID! Profits don't mount up as quickly, but risk is dramatically reduced.

Also, an additional warning if you grow your business into the commodity markets. Some commodities have LIMIT MOVES where the market will lock limit up or down and you can't get out after days of extreme losses. Some commodity traders are so fearful of the always-present possibility of limit moves that they deal in COMMODITY OPTIONS only, where margin calls and limit moves are effectively nipped in the bud and totally eliminated (See "INSURANCE" chapter coming up).

I've asked the question of numerous commodity futures and Forex gurus, *"How much can a trader afford to safely fund their account?!"* You don't want to bet the farm so this question is of utmost importance.

I've always been stunned at the silence in response. I know supposed experts charging thousands of dollars for their seminars yet in the end their students are no better off than when they began.

I was testing the *"Gurus"* who ALL failed my test. The answer is very simple.

The Worry Free Wealth Ratio

Not only do beginning traders start with too little money in their account but even when they adequately fund their trading it's often too much compared to their worth or how much money they make. I've spent a lot of time and research to come up with a very easy solution to this problem. I call this trading secret the worry free wealth ratio…

Step 1: Don't allow your needs expenses to exceed 50% of your total **after-tax income**. **Needs** expenses are the things you'd have to pay to keep a roof over your head, and food and drink in your belly, at the bare comfort level.

Step 2: Set aside 30% of your after-tax income to have **fun** during the year. You can't live an austere monastic lifestyle or you'll go crazy. Celebrate your earnings and have some fun.

Step 3: Always **save** 20% of your after-tax income and use it to (a) pay off your debts (b) build a balanced portfolio in stocks, bonds, and commodities, and (c) use a small portion to fund your futures trading account— adequate **savings** are vital to every traders success.

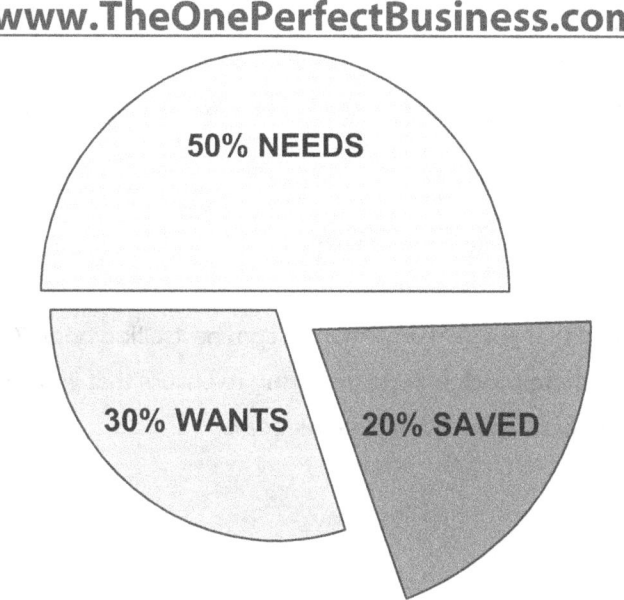

Let me explain imagining that you make $100,000 after-tax as an example.

By following the three steps above you would save $20,000. Of that money you should set aside ¼ to pay off your (a) credit card debt and (b) mortgage debt on your principal residence — that's $5,000. To simplify I'm assuming you've paid off all your debt.

The 70/30 Rule

Economist Bob Shiller at Yale looked at returns to bondholders, stock holders, and real estate investors since 1873. He found average returns after inflation to real estate investors — in terms of buying and holding — were exactly zero, about 2½% for bond investors, and about 7% for stock holders.

For this reason you should put 70% of your money in a balanced *"set it and forget"* portfolio that leans heavily toward stocks.

The best **set-and-forget** stock portfolio out there is **The Gone Fishing Portfolio** by Alex Green. You can learn all about this portfolio by ordering Alex's book on

Amazon.com. Seventy percent of the $20,000 you'd save in this example should go into the Gone Fishing Portfolio — that's $14,000 every year if your income remained the same.

Amazon Link: http://tinyurl.com/23a7shf

I also recommend that you read my Amazon.com bestselling book, **The Worry Free Wealth Guide to Stock Market Investing** to ensure that you have enough of a background to really understand what Alex says.

Amazon Link: http://tinyurl.com/27w6gvk

What about the 30% left over?

The answer depends on your investing ability. If you're new to investing you should put 100% of your savings into the Gone Fishing Portfolio just to get used to the idea of managing your own money.

Set up a Roth or Standard IRA and deposit your savings. If you save more than the maximum contribution put the rest in an individual investing account. For online stock investing I really like Scottrade.com, Fidelity.com, Etrade.com, or TDAmeritrade.com.

Use a demo account to practice trading futures with the Track n' Trade Live platform. Don't start trading futures with cash until you're very competent after **Monte Carlo** trading and have shown a consistent profit for at least 6 to 12 months.

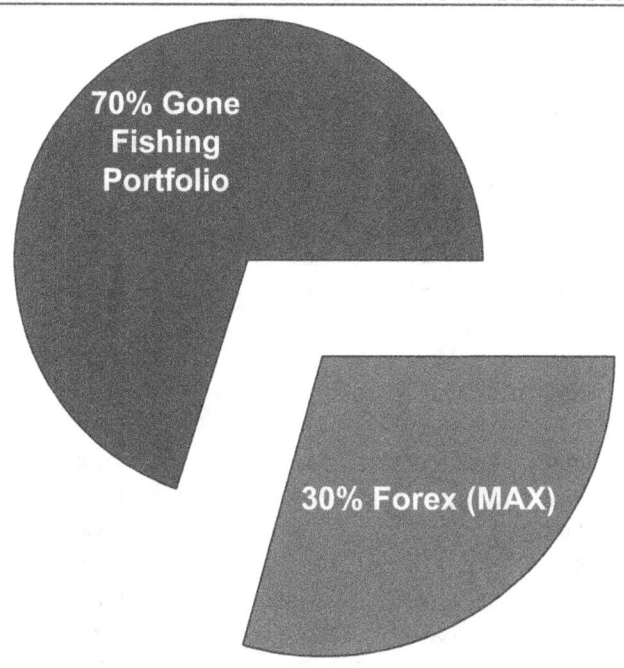

	Worry Free Wealth Ratio				
	Income Allocation			Savings Allocation	
Net Income	**50% Needs**	**30% Fun**	**20% Savings**	**70% Gone Fishin' Portfolio**	30% Trading*
$ 20,000	$ 10,000	$ 6,000	$ 4,000	$ 2,800	$ 1,200
$ 30,000	$ 15,000	$ 9,000	$ 6,000	$ 4,200	$ 1,800
$ 40,000	$ 20,000	$ 12,000	$ 8,000	$ 5,600	$ 2,400
$ 50,000	$ 25,000	$ 15,000	$ 10,000	$ 7,000	$ 3,000
$ 60,000	$ 30,000	$ 18,000	$ 12,000	$ 8,400	$ 3,600
$ 70,000	$ 35,000	$ 21,000	$ 14,000	$ 9,800	$ 4,200
$ 80,000	$ 40,000	$ 24,000	$ 16,000	$ 11,200	$ 4,800
$ 90,000	$ 45,000	$ 27,000	$ 18,000	$ 12,600	**$ 5,000**
$ 100,000	$ 50,000	$ 30,000	$ 20,000	$ 14,000	**$ 5,000**
$ 110,000	$ 55,000	$ 33,000	$ 22,000	$ 15,400	**$ 5,000**
$ 120,000	$ 60,000	$ 36,000	$ 24,000	$ 16,800	**$ 5,000**
$ 130,000	$ 65,000	$ 39,000	$ 26,000	$ 18,200	**$ 5,000**
$ 140,000	$ 70,000	$ 42,000	$ 28,000	$ 19,600	**$ 5,000**
$ 150,000	$ 75,000	$ 45,000	$ 30,000	$ 21,000	**$ 5,000**
$ 160,000	$ 80,000	$ 48,000	$ 32,000	$ 22,400	**$ 5,000**
$ 170,000	$ 85,000	$ 51,000	$ 34,000	$ 23,800	**$ 5,000**
$ 180,000	$ 90,000	$ 54,000	$ 36,000	$ 25,200	**$ 5,000**
$ 190,000	$ 95,000	$ 57,000	$ 38,000	$ 26,600	**$ 5,000**
$ 200,000	$ 100,000	$ 60,000	$ 40,000	$ 28,000	**$ 5,000**
$ 210,000	$ 105,000	$ 63,000	$ 42,000	$ 29,400	**$ 5,000**
$ 220,000	$ 110,000	$ 66,000	$ 44,000	$ 30,800	**$ 5,000**
$ 230,000	$ 115,000	$ 69,000	$ 46,000	$ 32,200	**$ 5,000**
$ 240,000	$ 120,000	$ 72,000	$ 48,000	$ 33,600	**$ 5,000**
$ 250,000	$ 125,000	$ 75,000	$ 50,000	$ 35,000	**$ 5,000**
$ 260,000	$ 130,000	$ 78,000	$ 52,000	$ 36,400	**$ 5,000**
$ 270,000	$ 135,000	$ 81,000	$ 54,000	$ 37,800	**$ 5,000**
$ 280,000	$ 140,000	$ 84,000	$ 56,000	$ 39,200	**$ 5,000**
$ 290,000	$ 145,000	$ 87,000	$ 58,000	$ 40,600	**$ 5,000**
$ 300,000	$ 150,000	$ 90,000	$ 60,000	$ 42,000	**$ 5,000**
$ 310,000	$ 155,000	$ 93,000	$ 62,000	$ 43,400	**$ 5,000**
$ 320,000	$ 160,000	$ 96,000	$ 64,000	$ 44,800	**$ 5,000**
$ 330,000	$ 165,000	$ 99,000	$ 66,000	$ 46,200	**$ 5,000**
$ 340,000	$ 170,000	$ 102,000	$ 68,000	$ 47,600	**$ 5,000**
$ 350,000	$ 175,000	$ 105,000	$ 70,000	$ 49,000	**$ 5,000**

* Do not risk more than $5,000 in Forex. Commodities (futures) requires more money — as I teach at
http://www.tradementors.com/ —but never risk more than 30% maximum of your savings in futures even once you are well trained. In your first 3 months to a year of you intial training as a Forex or futures trader it might even be wise for you to put 100% of your savings into the Gone Fishin' Portfolio as you simulation trade.

Never Re-Fund Your Futures Trading Account More Than 2 Years In A Row

Once you know you're a competent Forex trader you can use 30% ($1,000 is BEST but never risk more than up to a maximum of $5,000) of your **savings** no more than 3 years in a row to fund your trading account. If you're making a hundred grand net and saving $20k this works out to $6,000 — more than the $5,000 max you need. But here's the catch…

If you blow out year after year for 3 years stop!

If this happens there's something seriously wrong with your trading. So take the opportunity in those first few years to let my course (over at http://www.tradementors.com/) sink in. Also make sure you voraciously study the books that I recommend.

Finally we have studies in academic finance that show that Forex traders generally regard themselves as above average. This comes from our very dangerous human tendency to overestimate our individual achievements and abilities in relation to others.

How Can All Investors Be Above Average?

If you listened to Garrison Keillor's National Public radio show A *"Prairie Home Companion,"* you'll remember Lake Wobegon, where *"all the women are strong, all the men are good looking, and all the children are above average."* The **Lake Wobegon** effect where all, or nearly all of a group claim to be above average, has been observed among drivers, futures traders, Forex traders, stock day traders, stock investors, option traders, CEOs, stock market analysts, college students, parents, and even state education officials.

If you come into these markets thinking that you're automatically a better trader than everybody else you'll be your own worst enemy. You won't study the markets diligently, or enough, to have an edge when you decide to put your money on the line. You'll trade too frequently instead of waiting for *"prime"* opportunities that come along infrequently even for the best position trader. Or you won't spend enough time carefully Monte Carlo testing your autopilot settings as a mechanical trader (at http://www.tradementors.com/ you'll learn how to program the computer yourself to trade for you).

Higher Accuracy Reduces Capital Requirements

My favorite futures trader is Stanley Kroll. He's my favorite not just because he was an incredible trader but also because he was a kind person. Plus he published books methodically detailing step-by-step how to he became wealthy as a futures trader.

Amazon Link: http://tinyurl.com/2fh7oyg

Stanley was so skilled at market entry that he could get a successful entry in as little as 2 tries. Mathematically that's a 50% money management rule as I teach you at http://www.tradementors.com/

This means that if you master profitable entry and exit strategies you can trade on a lot less capital.

CHAPTER EIGHT: The Big Mac Index

The "*Law of One Price*" says that the same thing (stock share, futures contract, or Forex lot) can't trade at different prices on different exchanges — arbitrage selling and buying forces one price.

You can also apply the law of one price to consumer prices between two countries. This is called the theory of **PURCHASING POWER PARITY** (PPP). Here the exchange rate between currencies of two countries should be equal to the ratio of the inflation levels. This idea is from brilliant British financier David Ricardo from the 1800s.

As usual I'll use the EUR/USD pair to explain this...

The whole thing here is that the exchange rate should be such that something you consume in the United States should have the same price in Europe. A good example is McDonalds which operates highly standardized restaurant operations in 119 countries worldwide.

This means that a Big Mac in the euro-zone is exactly the same Big Mac hamburger in the United States!

So if the exchange rate is $1.4568 USD/EUR and a Big Mac costs $2.45 USD in the United States than it should cost €1.68 EUR in Europe. That's because 1.4568 USD/EUR = 0.6864 EUR/USD. And $2.45 USD X 0.6864 EUR/USD = €1.68 EUR

These numbers make it easy for you to set up the mathematical relationship David Ricardo saw a couple of hundred years ago. Purchasing Power Parity simply says that any consumer good should cost exactly the same whether you buy it with fistful of dollars in the United States or Euros in Germany!

If the price of a Big Mac is too high in Europe then the Euro should DROP to equal things out. It the price of a Big Mac is too high in America PPP says that the Euro should rise to compensate. Purchasing Power Parity forces commodity prices to be the same in each country of a trading pair when measured in either currency.

This is also called the *"absolute version of Purchasing Price Parity (PPP)."*

Burgers Without Borders — The Best Long Term Forex Indicator!

Did the movie *"Super Size Me"* leave you with a bad feeling about your urge to eat a Big Mac? Well let me show you a way to turn the battle of your bulge into windfall profits. PPP means a mouth watering Big Mac in the euro-zone should cost exactly the same as a hamburger in the United States!

If it doesn't that tells you something important!

The nice thing about Purchasing Power Parity (PPP) is that it can help you get an idea of what the equilibrium Forex rate should be in the pair you're trading. The Economist magazine each year compiles local prices of Big Macs around the world and calculates purchasing price parity based on "*Big Mac*" prices worldwide on all of the G7 and G10 trading pairs. It also gives you the exchange rate that makes the hamburger prices between America and elsewhere equal. Then it compares the implied PPP rate to the actual rate to see if there is a violation of purchasing power parity.

Look at the last column in the table on the next page. If a hamburger has a negative number in the euro-zone that means the currency is undervalued (-) and the EUR should appreciate. If the Big Mac is overvalued (+) in the eurozone the EUR should depreciate.

The Big Mac PPP Index For The EUR/USD Pair					
	Big Mac Prices		Implied	Actual	Valuation
	In Local	In USD	PPP of USD	Forex Rate	against USD
USD (2009)	$3.22	$3.22	----	----	----
Euro-zone (2009)	€3.42	$4.38	1.04 USD/EUR	1.28 USD/EUR	+24
USD (2008)	$3.57	$3.57	----	----	----
Euro-zone (2008)	€3.37	$5.34	1.06 USD/EUR	1.59 USD/EUR	+50
USD (2007)	$3.57	$3.57	----	----	----
Euro-zone (2007)	€2.94	$3.82	1.10 USD/EUR	1.30 USD/EUR	+19
USD (2006)	$3.10	$3.10	----	----	----
Euro-zone (2006)	€2.94	$3.77	1.05 USD/EUR	1.28 USD/EUR	+22
USD (2005)	$3.06	$3.06	----	----	----
Euro-zone (2005)	€3.58	$1.05	----	----	+17
USD (2004)	$2.90	$2.90	----	----	----
Euro-zone (2004)	€3.28	$1.06	----	----	+13
USD (2003)	$2.71	$2.71	----	----	----
Euro-zone (2003)	€2.71	$2.97	----	----	+10
USD (2002)	$2.54	$2.54	----	----	----
Euro-zone (2002)	€2.57	$2.27	0.93 USD/EUR	0.89 USD/EUR	-5
USD (2001)	$2.49	$2.49	----	----	----
Euro-zone (2001)	€2.67	$2.37	0.99 USD/EUR	0.88 USD/EUR	-11
USD (2000)	$2.51	$2.51	----	----	----
Euro-zone (2000)	€2.56	$2.37	0.98 USD/EUR	0.93 USD/EUR	-5
USD (1999)	$2.43	$2.43	----	----	----
Euro-zone (1999)	€2.52	$2.71	0.97 USD/EUR	1.08 USD/EUR	+11

You can chart this using a simple spreadsheet like Excel. This helps you see the extremes more clearly…

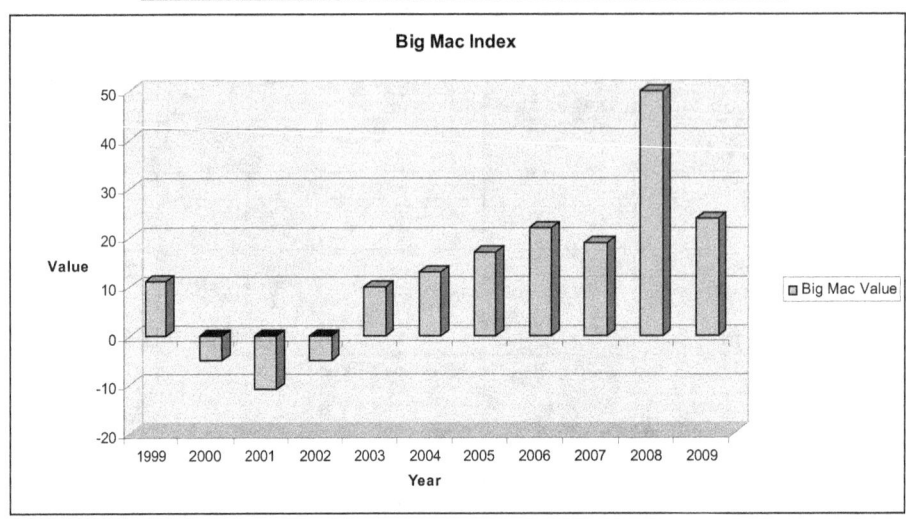

So the Big Mac Index says that the market should turn UPWARD in 2001 and DOWNWARD in 2008. Let's see what actually happened…

The simple graph above really gives you X-ray vision into Forex movements on a Monthly chart! In How to Master Forex Trading, it doesn't matter **what's** happening, or **why!** All we need is **activity…**

150

My **academics colleagues** who know of the Big Mac index don't know what's going on even when it's going on because the NEVER look at a long term chart in conjunction with the Big Mac index.

In all the time I've been into my http://www.tradementors.com/ *"investment spectrum"* series of *"currency expert"* interviews (and I've seen **hundreds** of them), **not one has ever mentioned** the Big Mac Index!!! Creating and maintaining a Big Mac chart is very simple, but can be extremely lucrative.

A Big Mac Index Chart is simply the level of the **Big Mac index** graphed in relation to the year. You should do this for every pair you follow that trades against the U.S. Dollar.

You are looking for extremes; an extreme **positive** value says that the foreign currency should **weaken**. An extremely **negative** value means that the U.S. Dollar should **strengthen**.

FUNDAMENTAL: Without consumer prices there could never be Forex prices!

Go long (buy a direct quote currency) when you expect foreign consumer prices to advance. Go short (sell a direct quote currency pair) when you expect foreign consumer prices to decline.

Direct quotes are where a foreign currency is the base pair against the U.S. Dollar — EUR/USD, AUD/USD, NZD/USD, etc…

Consumer prices act like a kind of a "*rubber band*" in relation to futures prices. If a foreign currency price is well above consumer prices, expect consumer prices to pull the foreign currency price back down, etcetera. A Big Mac index chart shows you immediately if you would be overpaying or underpaying for the Forex pair, and, as we've seen, this information can be **vital** to profitable positions.

Your Big Mac Index chart can be your "*crystal ball*" that every trader wishes for; you'll find yourself aware of **major moves** in prices **long before** many other traders catch on!

The story goes that Bernard Baruch abandoned all his stock market activities just before the 1929 crash when a shoeshine boy offered him a "*hot tip*" on a stock. Baruch reasoned that if somebody as green behind the ears as a shoeshine boy felt they understood the stock market that it was time to get out — the market was too hyped up.

That's easy for stocks but much harder in Forex for most people. Because they don't know about the Big Mac Index!

CHAPTER NINE: The World's Most Powerful Indicator

Change is the one simple law you can count on in this world. This is the driving force behind the **fact** that, "*What goes up must come down.*" In How to Master Forex Trading, we don't care **which way** prices are moving, only that they're moving, and this movement is called **momentum.**

Our mini lots need momentum to duplicate and multiply whether we pyramid, buy most of our mini lots at the beginning of the move, or more safely pillar our businesses!

Every Forex Pair has **only one highest point** and **only one lowest point** during each year or decade. If you could pick **just these two levels**, you would very quickly become the richest person in the world! If you knew a certain Forex pair's highest level, you would **sell** a mini lot (**knowing** the price could only go down from there!). **You wouldn't even need a stop loss!**, then you could sit, wait, and rake in the profits as the price eventually reached the lowest point.

Then you would take a massive profit and, **knowing** the price could only go up from that lowest level, **buy** a contract, sit back again and watch your margin account grow! That would be wonderful, but it's **not** likely to happen. The chances of your pinpointing **the one "*top*"** or **the one "*bottom*"** each year are **one in over 200 trading days** — not something to build a phenomenal business on.

There is a technique to use for spotting major market tops and bottoms. When used in conjunction with the other tools you've been introduced to in this How to Master Forex Trading program, can raise your business success rate to the 70-90% level. Numbers our members commonly trade at http://www.tradementors.com/

This Fundamental technique is called "*The Bulls and the Bears Red Light Green Light System.*"

Remember the long term moving average I introduced you to at the beginning of this program? It had an uncanny 80% success rate. But, it had a few false signals to.

The Bulls and the Bears system is a radical improvement over the long term moving average. This is a computer program that gives you an up arrow to buy or down arrow to sell. Let's look again at the EUR/USD that had 10 signals with a long term moving average on the monthly chart.

The Bulls and the Bears filters the 10 signals down to 5. Count the red arrows in the chart above to see this. When you add in the Big Mac indicator you end up with just two signals on the monthly chart.

For instance I noticed in 2008 that the Big Mac index was highly positive. But I missed the 08' top. As the market reacted into a new uptrend I waited for a down arrow to go short. On December 8th I got the signal and entered with a stop 225 PIPs behind. That has been a very profitable trade anybody could afford...

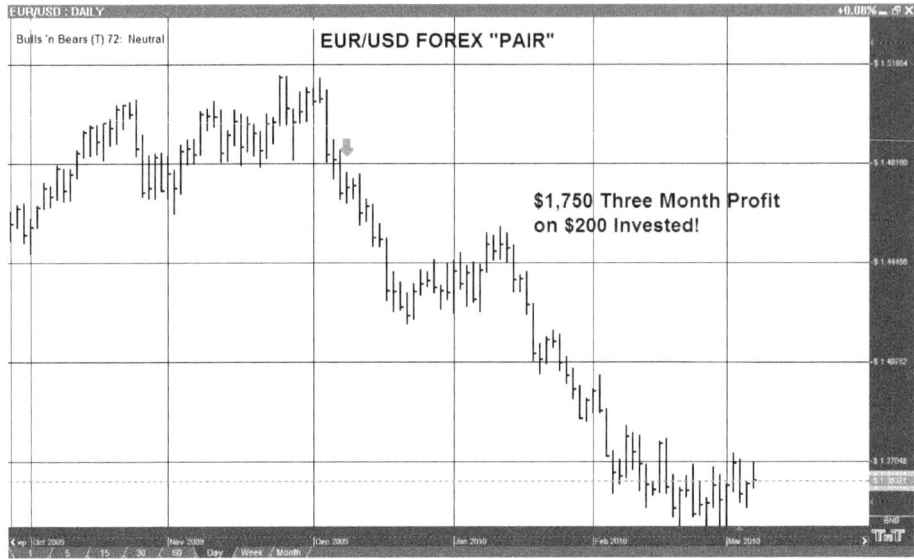

What's great about this trade is that since my crystal ball (the Big Mac Index) says that the major trend should continue down I can continue pillaring in that direction…

This brings us to another FUNDAMENTAL RULE: **Never** pillar when trading counter to the major trend on the monthly chart!

By the way, every tool you've learned is a version of the trend break I taught you at the very beginning of this course!

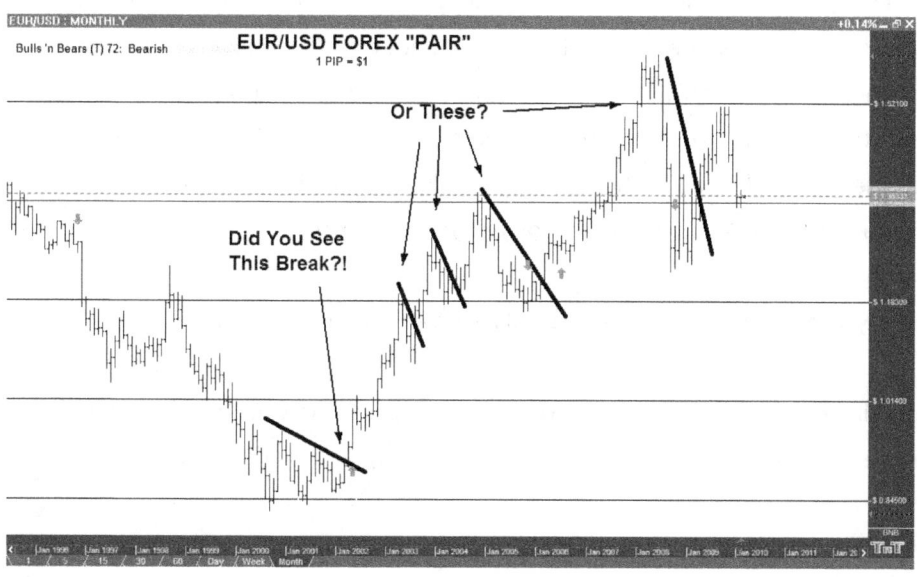

CHAPTER TEN: Insurance

What if you could buy insurance on a new enterprise you were considering before you jumped in to business? You would simply pay for it in "premium" as a good faith deposit guaranteeing you the **right** but not the **obligation**, to purchase your business at a pre-set future date. If the business explodes for others who bought in outright, you jump in! If it stinks, bringing in less money than the cost of doing business, you'd let your option go, and lose just the small premium you paid as compared to what you'd have lost buying in at full price.

This type of opportunity is commonplace in real estate.

Imagine you find a **hidden** deal. You investigate and discover that the owner has moved to Japan, needs to sell the property quickly, and is asking $90,000.

You're study and analysis indicates his home is really worth $150,000 and, **with a little time**, you believe you can find a buyer at $150,000 or $125,000 absolute minimum.

Normally you'd have to go through the hassles to buy the house outright before you sell it; new financing, not to mention the stress of reselling the property while you make mortgage payments. So you talk to the seller's local real estate broker offering $1,000 cash for a **90 day option**. In essence, you're saying, "*I'd like to lock in the* **right** *to buy this property for $90,000 within 90 days. If I don't, however, I'm under no obligation to buy and only lose my $1,000 cash.*"

Why would you risk $1,000?

You'd do it to stand, to make a $60,000 profit on a $1,000 investment. That's a 6,000% return in 90 days, (24,000% annualized), **if** you find a buyer at $150,000 in 90 days.

Leverage is the "*secret*" behind these eye popping returns!

You've also been marketing for buyers and think you can sell it for that price, so you pay the **premium** ($1,000), take on the **risk**, and look for a buyer to make your deal work.

Imagine that you find your buyer within 90 days, with a large down-payment, who also qualifies for a new loan for the balance above the down-payment. Both the down-payment and loan proceeds are deposited into escrow so that you can use the cash to **exercise your option** to buy the property for $100,000 and immediately resell it for $150,000. Commissions and fees are paid out to the realtor, appraiser, and banker, and you walk away with, say, a net $40,000 profit. That $40,000 on your $1,000 *"premium,"* which is *"only"* (16,000% annualized)!'

P. T. Barnum taught, *"Engage in one kind of business only, and stick to it faithfully until you succeed, or until your experience shows that you should abandon it."*

You should be systematic in any business you start. This real estate speculator (businessman) did his homework, established a plan, took action, put himself at the top of his **own pyramid** (not someone else's) by levering $150,000 with just $1,000, and used that option to generate a 16,000% profit within 90 days. Intelligent? Yes. Canny? Yes. *"Chancy?"* Yes. Something you could do? Absolutely. Have you done it? Not likely. How come? The huge amount of time and effort to make the deal happen. There's also the **huge uncertainty** that worries you: "What happens ***if*** I can't find a buyer at $150,000?" You'd have to **study**, research, plan, and determine what the **likelihood** of finding a buyer for the property really is.

What if the **big if** of coming up with the buyer could be eliminated? You're leaning forward with interest now…

Futures currency options are **exactly the same** as the example above, but better! You spot a *"hidden, opportunity"* pay the option premium (which is **all** your risk —

159

guaranteeing you won't lose more), and if the Forex pair moves the way you expect, you exercise your option (do the deal) and reap your profits. The buyer problem is very real in real estate. But it's rarely a problem in the currency futures markets because of vast liquidity!

If you've really been paying attention, you might be thinking, "*I wonder if I could make a lot of money selling overpriced options!*" Yes. But if you want to go in that direction I strongly recommend you join my trading club at

http://www.tradementors.com/

In closing here's the set of rules I follow to guide my own personal trading (yes I do trade!)…

…**MAKE AN INTENSE STUDY OF TECHNICAL ANALYSIS.** I've shown you how powerful a long-term moving average, trend break, and the Bulls n' the Bears system is. Now it's up to you to make this information yours through diligent study to convince yourself that all of this really works. You can't act on what you don't believe, and you can't believe what you don't study for yourself.

…**STUDY THE DIVERSE FUNDAMENTAL FACTORS THAT AFFECT EACH CURRENCY.** Believe it or not just your understanding of the Big Mac Index alone puts you head and shoulders above 95% of Forex traders. Yet there are other fundamental factors you need to pay attention to and master such as the **Trade Balance Trend Analysis** and **Uncovered Interest Parity**. These are refinements I mentor you through in the premiere Forex trading club at http://www.tradementors.com/

…**TRADE TO MAKE LOTS OF MONEY FAST.** The only use to you that these markets have is to take a small amount of money and grow it fast. As you build large equity positions move your big profits over to a passive equity strategy with a fast doubling rate. The best I have found is **The Gone Fishing Portfolio** by Alex Green (get his book at Amazon.com). Don't hang around these markets too long if you break the million mark. My friend and colleague Fred Rouse, Ph.D. did so with disastrous results. He took a few thousand dollars, turned it into over two million, hung around and lost it all back! Maintain a *"hit and run"* mentality in these markets!!!

…**TRADE AS LITTLE AS POSSIBLE.** People who are desperate or trade for excitement over-trade in these markets. This means that they don't wait for the best odds and come out guaranteed losers!

...IDENTIFY THE MAJOR AND MINOR TREND AND TRADE ONLY FOR THE BIG MOVES. I can't tell you how many folks come into these markets thinking that killer opportunities come along every day. This just isn't so. By focusing on the major trend and then *"drilling down"* to the entry and exit triggers on the daily chart you'll automatically be ahead of the game.

...KEEP THINGS SIMPLE. What works best in these markets is a **simple trend following system approach.** Don't ever forget that. Strive to keep your market research and trading campaigns simple. Don't use too many indicators or over think and second guess. If you can do this you'll start to see what really works over time and will be amazed by the simplicity. Trust me since I am the guy with the Ph.D. in financial complexity!

...DEVELOP AND PRACTICE PATIENCE, OBJECTIVITY, COURAGE, AND DETERMINATION. This is not a game of *"who's who"* or *"who's cool."* Its a game of who wins and who survives. A big part of that is developing a cold blooded, mercenary mentality when it comes to the markets. Believe it or not, if you can develop this attitude through practice it will help you in managing money in all other parts of your life.

...STAY ON BOARD WINNING TRADES. Never close trades due to boredom or impatience because you think you should be winning more. This invariably happens when the market *"stalls"* before turning a winning trade into a spectacular trade. Loser traders have a tendency to jump out at the wrong time instead of letting the market take them out of the trade.

...WHEN YOU'RE WRONG SHOOT FOR A DRAW OR A SMALL PROFIT. Never try to get back at the market. When you know in your gut that you're wrong about the market and shouldn't be in a trade strive to exit gracefully. Losers have a tendency to hold their losing trades and cut their *"would have been"* really profitable winner trades short — that's exactly why we call these folks **LOSERS**.

...**STOP TRADING IF YOU ARE LOSING MORE THAN 50% OF THE TIME**. You CANNOT win if you lose on more than half of your trades. If you find that this is so STOP trading temporarily. It's time for you to regroup and rethink your strategy. You should be thinking about trading less, being more patient, more discriminating at all times to zero in on high win probability trades; in so doing you'll be winning more than 50% of the time. If not you're doing something wrong and need to regroup and recalibrate!

...**DECIDE WHICH BUSINESS** (Forex Pair) you would like to go into first as a beginner — generally speaking I consider the EUR/USD pair best for beginners.

 ...**PRE-DETERMINE** (Plan, Plan, Plan!) the price at which you'll enter this business as determined by your **planning**, utilizing monthly, weekly, and daily charts with the tools I've taught you in this course.

...**PRE-PLAN** the amount of capital you can commit to Forex and futures using the Worry Free Wealth Ratio and 70/30 savings rule.

...**PRE-SET** your stop-loss points and instruct the Track n' Trade Live Forex platform to establish these WHEN YOUR ORIGINAL LOT IS BOUGHT OR SOLD. Do not allow your stop-loss to lose more than 225 PIPs as a hard and fast rule per mini-lot in your initial $1,000 account.

...**PRE-SELECT** a point at which you will **end your business** — after $1,000 profit? $2,000, $5,000, $15,000? Or will you let the price momentum, stop-loss, or a reversing Bulls n' Bears arrow decide for you automatically? Bulls n' Bears reverse is my favorite!

...**MAJOR MOVES** are what we trade, **not** daily fluctuations (this is called *"day trading"* and it results in tremendous losses for most traders — unless done mechanically). Compulsive gamblers tend to day-trade!

… **DEVELOP YOUR COMMON SENSE.** Common sense is the least common trait of our population. You have to learn to think for yourself. This isn't taught in the university. In fact, as a university professor myself I know of no way to teach it. Learn to spot special profit opportunities developing by watching your price graphs and listening to the world about you.

…**MAKE SUCCESS A HABIT.** To manage your success you must learn what success in Forex feels like! In How to Master Forex Trading, you can experience **reality** — **MONTE CARLO SIMULATE** before you ever open a Forex margin account! *"Everything s/he touches turns to gold,"* simply says that someone has developed the **habit** of succeeding. Success is a habit, **it must be learned**.

…**GO SLOWLY.** An elephant is eaten one bit at a time and Rome wasn't built in a day! *"But it all starts with the first bite and the first day."* Here, now, a great opportunity has fallen into your lap. Organize your day with a list of tasks making the highest priority just 15-30 minutes of study each day of what you've learned in this program. I explain to my MBA students that Albert Einstein flatly stated that anybody with a functional brain can soon become an **expert** in any field if he or she would simply study that subject only 15 minutes a day! You don't need to run out and enroll in an MBA to learn to trade. You don't have to sacrifice your time from what you love to do, neglect your family, risk rent money, tap your savings, borrow from your credit cards, or spend your whole life insurance cash value!

All HOW TO MASTER FOREX TRADING requires is 15-30 minutes a day to prove itself to you and to demonstrate that the concepts in this program are sound, that they actually work — and will work for you, too!

Just 15-30 minutes a day to reach a lifestyle of leisure where you determine how and when you use your time as the master of your destiny. In fact, if you become one of the 5% at the top of this business your only financial concern will be how to spend and preserve the wealth you've accumulated!

Just try to prove me wrong!

CHAPTER TWELVE: "*The Secret*" To Success — Focus and Perseverance!

When you learned to drive a car you had to learn much **before** you jumped in the driver's seat! Then you started driving and probably scared yourself a few time by going faster than should have around a few dangerous curves. These "*practical experiences*" are the "*dues*" that **had to be paid** to achieve your goal of becoming a competent driver.

Bodybuilders, for instance, don't get **any benefit** from their effort until they make their muscles work to "*failure.*" That can take numerous repetitive movements and heavy weights over many years as dues!

RECOGNIZE WHERE YOU WANT TO GO, TAKE FOCUSED ACTION, AND PERSERVERE, AND YOU'LL REACH YOUR GOALS.

If you're financial impoverished, if you haven't got something in your life you truly need — whatever it is — that you've not obtained, you've missed the boat on your way by not recognizing opportunities that would have manifested your heart's desires.

WHAT THE MIND CAN CONCIEVE IT CAN ACHIEVE! Say's Napoleon Hill.

You're mind has been miss-conceiving for too long. The **fantastic truth** is that opportunity abounds whether you decide to recognize it or not. By changing your mind you'll see that there really is more than enough for everybody. That's what **How to Master Forex Trading** is all about.

You may believe in competition which directly implies that you see a world of limited resources where "*some have to lose since there's just not enough to go around*"and so on. That's what CEOs and their paid-off politicians (who don't feel inflation personally since they live off of your taxes — none of which are ever laid off and unemployed), the media, and many religions want you to think, but THAT

KIND OF BELEIF IS SHOCKINGLY WRONG! This program has meticulously explained to you why this is such a disgraceful lie!

The only obstructions holding you back from all you want come from you. I know that is a strong statement but your barriers to wealth aren't made by the Cosmos. I know this is true because everywhere you observe; the Cosmos is plentiful — super abundant in fact.

Did you know that the Midwest of the United States has enough productive capacity to feed the world several times over each year? Why does the U.S. federal government pay farmers to **not** grow crops? The only possibility is a widely held stinking thinking belief in lack in lieu of abundance.

If you change your thinking from lack to abundance other people in your life will **instantly** benefit — that's the basic law of the mind. That's the way your mind really works when you use it right! If you were to enjoy life by partaking in all the richness of this world who could you possibly injure?

What now? Will you take **ACTION** on what you've learned in How to Master Forex Trading? Or will this course sit gathering dust on a shelf or as a PDF sitting on your computer drive with other courses you acquired with hope and excitement but never employed…more potential unrealized.

A big part of the reason I am successful today is that I promised my wife 17 years ago that *"If I buy a course, I study, and thoroughly internalize the course."* Ironically, you are benefiting from that commitment since many of the tools you've just learned would have taken you a decade or more to figure out alone — I know since I did it for you.

Is your life heading in the direction you want? Are you contented, as wealthy as you wish? Affluence is a **condition** of life, not a dollar figure in your bank account. Did you ever ponder that money is not what people want? People yearn for what money buys: food, shelter, healthcare, entertainment, travel, helping those you love, and financially supporting those near you in need. There's **nothing whatsoever** shameful in wanting all of these delightful benefits only money can buy. These longings are the unconscious you trying to express How to Master Forex Trading.

Yet only you can get in your way.

I had a problem about money for the longest time throughout my twenties and much of my thirties. I kept going from *"get rich quick scheme to get rich quick scheme."* You know the type, the guy or gal that's well dressed, drives a nice car, is charismatic, has lots of exciting stories, and ideas to get rich but IS ALWAYS broke. I wanted all those material things to, *"show my family I had made it."* Marisol, my wife, told me, *"The day you STOP fretting over money is when you'll start accumulating all you desire and really need."* When that day came, sure enough, the money started rolling in.   And the projects I undertake today are all worthwhile and solid, NOT pipedreams and get rich quick schemes.

It all got better when I lost much of my prior emotional attachment to money by forgiving my frustrations with some help from **Spirit**!

We could all use a little more **Spirit** in our lives and a lot less frustration. I still like money but now I see it as an *"infinitely renewable resource"* from a cosmic faucet I turn on with my mind. The only obstacle standing between you and all you desire is a willingness to let go of everything holding you back depending on **the way you spend your time from now on**. That's all!

If you'll give this program 15-30 Minutes each and every day for the next 3 months, I assure you that this won't be the end of another useless course…It'll be…

THE START!

Give this **vital** message to your family, friends, and associates! They're barely treading water in a political-economy that could care less about their individual Right to Wealth!

Send them over to us to download this course in it's FREE COMPLETE electronic version at http://www.TheBestBusinessOnEarth.com!

GLOSSARY

Here are some commonly used terms that are useful for you to know. Come back and read it time to time to build your vocabulary and general understanding of Forex…

American Currency Quotation — A direct quotation in the foreign exchange markets whereby the value of the American dollar is stated as a per-unit measure of a foreign currency. This type of quotation shows how much U.S. currency it takes to purchase one unit of foreign currency. EUR/USD is an American Quotation.

Average True Range (ATR) — Developed by J. Welles Wilder and introduced in his book, New Concepts in Technical Trading Systems (1978), the Average True Range (ATR) indicator measures a security's volatility. As such, the indicator does not provide an indication of price direction or duration, simply the degree of price movement or volatility. This can be very effective for trailing stops.

Backspread — A type of options spread in which a trader holds more long positions than short positions. The premium collected from the sale of the short option is used to help finance the purchase of the long options. This type of spread enables the trader to have significant exposure to expected moves in the underlying asset while limiting the amount of loss in the event prices do not move in the direction the trader had hoped for. This spread can be created using either all call options or all put options.

Balance Of Payments – BOP — A record of all transactions made between one particular country and all other countries during a specified period of time. BOP compares the dollar difference of the amount of exports and imports, including all financial exports and imports. A negative balance of payments means that more money is flowing out of the country than coming in, and vice versa.

Balance Of Trade – BOT — The difference between a country's imports and its exports. Balance of trade is the largest component of a country's balance of payments. Debit items include imports, foreign aid, domestic spending abroad and domestic investments abroad. Credit items include exports, foreign spending in the domestic economy and foreign investments in the domestic economy. A country has a trade deficit if it imports more than it exports; the opposite scenario is a trade surplus. Also referred to as "trade balance" or "international trade balance."

Base Currency — The first currency quoted in a currency pair on Forex. It is also typically considered the domestic currency or accounting currency. For accounting purposes, a firm may use the base currency to represent all profits and losses. It is sometimes referred to as the "*primary currency*". For example, if you were looking at the CAD/USD currency pair, the Canadian dollar would be the base currency and the U.S. dollar would be the quote currency. The price represents how much of the quote currency is needed for you to get one unit of the base currency.

Big Mac PPP — A survey done by The Economist that determines what a country's exchange rate would have to be for a Big Mac in that country to cost the same as it does in the United States. Purchase power parity (PPP) is the theory that currencies adjust according to changes in their purchasing power. With the Big Mac PPP, purchasing power is reflected by the price of a McDonald's Big Mac in a particular country. The measure gives an impression of how overvalued or undervalued a currency is.

Blotter — A record of trades and the details of the trades made over a period of time (usually one trading day). The details of a trade will include such things as the time, price, order size and a specification of whether it was a buy or sell order. The blotter is usually created through a trading software program that records the trades made through a data feed. The purpose of a trade blotter is to carefully document the trades so that they can be reviewed and confirmed by the trader or the brokerage firm. The blotter is used in the stock market, foreign exchange market, and the bond market and can be customized based on the needs of the user.

Bretton Woods Agreement — A 1944 agreement made in Bretton Woods, New Hampshire, which helped to establish a fixed exchange rate in terms of gold for major currencies. The International Monetary Fund was also established at this time. This agreement governed currency relationships until the early 1970s, when a floating exchange rate system was adopted. Before its breakdown, the agreement was useful in maintaining order and accomplishing common objectives among the countries that created it.

Bull Put Spread — A type of options strategy that is used when the investor expects a moderate rise in the price of the underlying asset. This strategy is constructed by purchasing one put option while simultaneously selling another put option with a higher strike price. The goal of this strategy is realized when the price of the underlying stays above the higher strike price, which causes the short option to expire worthless, resulting in the trader keeping the premium. This type of strategy (writing one option and selling another with a higher strike price) is known as a credit spread because the amount received by selling the put option with a higher strike is more than enough to cover the cost of purchasing the put with the lower strike. The maximum possible profit using this strategy is equal to the difference between the amount received from the short put and the amount used to pay for the long put. The maximum loss a trader can incur when using this strategy is equal to the difference between the strike prices and the net credit received. Bull put spreads can be created with in-the-money or out-of-the-money put options, all with the same expiration date.

Cable — Slang used among Forex traders referring to the exchange rate between the U.S. dollar and the British pound sterling. Because it is the norm in Forex for most major currencies to be quoted against the U.S. dollar on a regular basis, "*cable*" is a commonly used term. "*Cable*" can also be used to refer simply to the

British pound sterling. For example, you may hear someone dealing with the Forex market saying, "*The cable is up today*," or, "*The cable has been trending lower lately*." The origins of this term are attributed to the fact that in the 1800s, the dollar/pound sterling exchange rate was transmitted via transatlantic cable. Forex brokers are sometimes referred to as "*cable dealers*".

Cambist — An expert trader who rapidly buys and sells currency throughout the day. The term comes from the Latin word "*cambiere*" which means "*to exchange*".

Cash Delivery

1. The same-day settlement of a currency trade in the **Forex market**. This means that delivery and settlement of the transaction occur on the same date that the currency trade is made. In order for this to occur, the Forex position must be opened and closed within the same trading day. As is the case with most financial markets, when you place an order in the Forex market, the trade is executed shortly afterward, but the settlement of trades - during which the trade details are entered into the books and records of the trading parties - typically occurs at a later time. Cash delivery is exceptional, because all of this happens in the same day.

2. In the context of **futures contracts**, a settlement term in a contract that stipulates that the underlying asset of the contract will not be delivered on the delivery date - rather, the net cash value of the position will be transferred to the applicable party instead. Rather than physically deliver the underlying commodity or asset to the contract holder, it is much easier to simply transact the net cash value of the futures position instead. This allows investors to hedge against price changes in the underlying asset without having to worry about physically taking delivery.

Commodity Block Currency — A currency that belongs to a country whose economy is strongly correlated with the price fluctuations of a certain commodity. For example, a large portion of the Canadian economy is tied to the price of oil, which causes the price of this commodity to become a major driver in the value of the Canadian dollar. Other countries such as Australia or New Zealand are in a similar position due to their economic dependence on precious metals such as gold. All of these countries have money flowing in when their respective commodities rise, causing their currencies to appreciate.

Constant Currencies — An exchange rate that eliminates the effects of exchange rate fluctuations and that is used when calculating financial performance numbers. Companies with major foreign operations often use constant currencies when calculating their yearly performance measures.

For example, consider a French company that sells primarily abroad and sets its prices according to U.S. dollars. If sales increase 10% in dollar terms, but the dollar fell 5% against the franc during the year, only a 5% increase in sales will be reported in the accounts, unless a constant currency is applied in the calculation. In other words, the use of constant currencies allows companies to show performance unaffected by currency fluctuations.

Crawling Peg — A system of exchange rate adjustment in which a currency with a fixed exchange rate is allowed to fluctuate within a band of rates. The par value of the stated currency is also adjusted frequently due to market factors such as inflation. This gradual shift of the currency's par value is done as an alternative to a sudden and significant devaluation of the currency. For example, in the 1990s, Mexico had fixed its peso with the U.S. dollar. However, due to the significant inflation in Mexico, as compared to the U.S., it was evident that the peso would need to be severely devalued. Because a rapid devaluation would create instability, Mexico put into place a crawling peg exchange rate adjustment system, and the peso was slowly devalued toward a more appropriate exchange rate.

Cross Currency — A pair of currencies traded in forex that does not include the U.S. dollar. One foreign currency is traded for another without having to first exchange the currencies into American dollars. Historically, an individual who wished to exchange a sum of money into a different currency would be required to first convert that money into U.S dollars, and then convert it into the desired currency; cross currencies help individuals and traders bypass this step. The GBP/JPY cross, for example, was invented to help individuals in England and Japan who wanted to convert their money directly without having to first convert it into U.S dollars.

Currency Basket — A selected group of currencies in which the weighted average is used as a measure of the value or the amount of an obligation. A currency basket functions as a benchmark for regional currency movements - its composition and weighting depends on its purpose. A currency basket is commonly used in contracts as a way of avoiding (or minimizing) the risk of currency fluctuations. The European currency unit (which was replaced by the euro) and the Asian currency unit are examples of currency baskets.

Currency Carry Trade — A strategy in which an investor sells a certain currency with a relatively low interest rate and uses the funds to purchase a different currency yielding a higher interest rate. A trader using this strategy attempts to capture the difference between the rates, which can often be substantial, depending on the amount of leverage used. Here's an example of a "yen carry trade": a trader borrows 1,000 Japanese yen from a Japanese bank, converts the funds into U.S. dollars and buys a bond for the equivalent amount. Let's assume that the bond pays 4.5% and the Japanese interest rate is set at 0%. The trader stands to make a profit of 4.5% as long as the exchange rate between the countries does not change. Many professional traders use this trade because the gains can become very large when leverage is taken into consideration. If the trader in our example uses a common leverage factor of 10:1, then she can stand to make a profit of 45%. The big risk in a carry trade is the uncertainty of exchange rates. Using the example above, if the U.S. dollar were to fall in value relative to the Japanese yen, then the trader would run the risk of losing money. Also, these transactions are generally done with a lot of leverage, so a small movement in exchange rates can result in huge losses unless the position is hedged appropriately.

Currency Convertibility — The ease with which a country's currency can be converted into gold or another currency. Convertibility is extremely important for international commerce. When a currency in inconvertible, it poses a risk and barrier to trade with foreigners who have no need for the domestic currency. Government restrictions can often result in a currency with a low convertibility. For example, a government with low reserves of hard foreign currency often restrict currency convertibility because the government would not be in a position to intervene in the foreign exchange market (i.e. revalue, devalue) to support their own currency if and when necessary.

Currency Forward — A forward contract in the Interbank Forex market that locks in the price at which an entity can buy or sell a currency on a future date. Also known as "*outright forward currency transaction*", "*forward outright*" or "*FX forward*". In currency forward contracts, the contract holders are obligated to buy or sell the currency at a specified price, at a specified quantity and on a specified future date. These contracts cannot be transferred.

Currency Futures — A transferable futures contract that specifies the price at which a specified currency can be bought or sold at a future date. Currency future contracts allow investors to hedge against foreign exchange risk. Since these contracts are marked-to-market daily, investors can--by closing out their position-- exit from their obligation to buy or sell the currency prior to the contract's delivery date.

Currency Option — A contract that grants the holder the right, but not the obligation, to buy or sell currency at a specified exchange rate during a specified period of time. For this right, a premium is paid to the broker, which will vary depending on the number of contracts purchased. Currency options are one of the best ways for corporations or individuals to hedge against adverse movements in exchange rates. Investors can hedge against foreign currency risk by purchasing a currency option put or call. For example, assume that an investor believes that the USD/EUR rate is going to increase from 0.80 to 0.90 (meaning

177

that it will become more expensive for a European investor to buy U.S dollars). In this case, the investor would want to buy a call option on USD/EUR so that he or she could stand to gain from an increase in the exchange rate (or the USD rise).

Currency Overlay — the outsourcing of currency risk management to a specialist firm, known as the overlay manager. This is used in international investment portfolios to separate the management of currency risk from the asset allocation and security selection decisions of the investor's money managers. The overlay manager's hedging is "overlaid" on the portfolios created by the other money managers, whose activities continue unaffected.

Currency Pair — The quotation and pricing structure of the currencies traded in the Forex market: the value of a currency is determined by its comparison to another currency. The first currency of a currency pair is called the "*base currency*", and the second currency is called the "*quote currency*". The currency pair shows how much of the quote currency is needed to purchase one unit of the base currency. All Forex trades involve the simultaneous buying of one currency and selling of another, but the currency pair itself can be thought of as a single unit, an instrument that is bought or sold. If you buy a currency pair, you buy the base currency and sell the quote currency. The bid (buy price) represents how much of the quote currency is needed for you to get one unit of the base currency. Conversely, when you sell the currency pair, you sell the base currency and receive the quote currency. The ask (sell price) for the currency pair represents how much you will get in the quote currency for selling one unit of base currency. For example, if the USD/EUR currency pair is quoted as being USD/EUR = 1.5 and you purchase the pair, this means that for every 1.5 euros that you sell, you purchase (receive) US$1. If you sold the currency pair, you would receive 1.5 euros for every US$1 you sell. The inverse of the currency quote is EUR/USD, and the corresponding price would be EUR/USD = 0.667, meaning that US$0.667 would buy 1 euro.

Currency Risk — A form of risk that arises from the change in price of one currency against another. Whenever investors or companies have assets or business operations across national borders, they face currency risk if their positions are not hedged. For example, if you are a U.S. investor and you have stocks in Canada, the return that you will realize is affected by both the change in the price of the stocks and the change in the value of the Canadian dollar against the U.S. dollar. So, if you realize a 15% return in your Canadian stocks but the Canadian dollar depreciates 15% against the U.S. dollar, this will amount to no gain at all. Academic studies of currency risk suggest - although without absolute certainty - that investors bearing currency risk are not compensated with higher potential returns, meaning it is essentially a needless risk to bear.

Currency Swap — A swap that involves the exchange of principal and interest in one currency for the same in another currency. It is considered to be a foreign exchange transaction and is not required by law to be shown on the balance sheet. For example, suppose a U.S.-based company needs to acquire Swiss francs and a Swiss-based company needs to acquire U.S. dollars. These two companies could arrange to swap currencies by establishing an interest rate, an agreed upon amount and a common maturity date for the exchange. Currency swap maturities are negotiable for at least 10 years, making them a very flexible method of foreign exchange. Currency swaps were originally done to get around exchange controls.

Current Account — The difference between a nation's total exports of goods, services and transfers, and its total imports of them. Current account balance calculations exclude transactions in financial assets and liabilities. The level of the current account is followed as an indicator of trends in foreign trade.

Current Account Deficit — Occurs when a country's total imports of goods, services and transfers is greater than the country's total export of goods, services and transfers. This situation makes a country a net debtor to the rest of the world. A substantial current account deficit is not necessarily a bad thing for certain countries. Developing counties may run a current account deficit in the short term to increase local productivity and exports in the future.

Daily Cut-Off — In the Forex market, a particular point in time specified by a Forex dealer to stand as the end of the current trading day and the beginning of a new trading day. This is done for primarily administrative and logistical reasons, because although the Forex market trades 24 hours a day, the market and its intermediaries require a specified beginning and end to each trading day in order to record trade dates and define settlement periods. For example, let's say a Forex dealer specified that the daily cut-off was 5pm every day, and a trader placed two Forex trades on the evening of January 1 - one at 4:50pm and another at 5:15pm. Since the daily cut-off is 5pm, the first trade would be booked as taking place on January 1, while the second would be recorded as a January 2 trade, since it took place after the daily cut-off.

Decentralized Market — A market structure that consists of a network of various technical devices that enable investors to create a marketplace without a centralized location. In a decentralized market, technology provides investors with access to various bids/ask prices and makes it possible for them to deal directly with other investors/dealers rather than with a given exchange. The foreign exchange market is an example of a decentralized market because there is no one physical location where investors go to buy or sell currencies. Forex traders can use the internet to check the quotes of various currency pairs from different dealers from around the world.

Deflation — A general decline in prices, often caused by a reduction in the supply of money or credit. Deflation can be caused also by a decrease in government, personal or investment spending. The opposite of inflation, deflation has the side effect of increased unemployment since there is a lower level of demand in the economy, which can lead to an economic depression. Central banks attempt to stop severe deflation, along with severe inflation, in an attempt to keep the excessive drop in prices to a minimum. The decline in prices of assets, is often known as Asset Deflation. Declining prices, if they persist, generally create a vicious spiral of negatives such as falling profits, closing factories, shrinking employment and incomes, and increasing defaults on loans by companies and individuals. To counter deflation, the Federal Reserve (the Fed) can use monetary policy to increase the money supply and deliberately induce rising prices, causing inflation. Rising prices provide an essential lubricant for any sustained recovery because businesses increase profits and take some of the depressive pressures off wages and debtors of every kind. Deflationary periods can be both short or long, relatively speaking. Japan, for example, had a period of deflation lasting decades starting in the early 1990's. The Japanese government lowered interest rates to try and stimulate inflation, to no avail. Zero interest rate policy was ended in July of 2006.

Devaluation — A deliberate downward adjustment to a country's official exchange rate relative to other currencies. In a fixed exchange rate regime, only a decision by a country's government (i.e central bank) can alter the official value of the currency. Contrast to "*revaluation*". There are two implications for a currency devaluation. First, devaluation makes a country's exports relatively less expensive for foreigners and second, it makes foreign products relatively more expensive for domestic consumers, discouraging imports. As a result, this may help to reduce a country's trade deficit.

Direct Quote — A foreign exchange rate quoted as the domestic currency per unit of the foreign currency. In other words, it involves quoting in fixed units of foreign currency against variable amounts of the domestic currency. For example, in the U.S., a direct quote for the Canadian dollar would be US$0.85 = C$1. Conversely, in Canada, a direct quote for U.S. dollars would be C$1.17 = US$1.

Dirty Float — A system of floating exchange rates in which the government or the country's central bank occasionally intervenes to change the direction of the value of the country's currency. In most instances, the intervention aspect of a dirty float system is meant to act as a buffer against an external economic shock before its effects become truly disruptive to the domestic economy.   For example, country X may find that some hedge fund is speculating that its currency will depreciate substantially, thus the hedge fund is starting to short massive amounts of country X's currency. Because country X uses a dirty float system, the government decides to take swift action and buy back a large amount of its currency in order to limit the amount of devaluation caused by the hedge fund. A dirty float system isn't considered to be a true floating exchange rate because, theoretically, true floating rate systems don't allow for intervention.

Dollar Drain — When a country imports more goods and services from another country than it exports back to the same country. The net effect of spending more money importing than is received from exporting causes a net reduction in the importing country's reserves of the exporting country's currency. For example, if Canada has exports $500 million worth of goods and services to the U.S. and has also imported $650 million worth of goods and services from the U.S., the net effect will be a reduction in Canada's U.S. dollar reserves. A dollar drain position should not be maintained indefinitely. As a result of the laws of supply and demand, importing more than is exported may cause a devaluation of the importing country's currency. However, this effect will be mitigated if foreign investors pour their money into the importing country's stocks and bonds, as these actions will increase the demand for the importing country's currency, causing it to appreciate in value.

Dual Exchange Rate — A situation in which there is a fixed official exchange rate and an illegal market-determined parallel exchange rate. The different exchange rates are used in different situations, either in exchanges or evaluations, as mandated by the government. Argentina adopted a dual exchange rate following its catastrophic economic troubles in the beginning of 2002. The illegal market-determined exchange rate would be preferred in a situation such as a cost-benefit analysis conducted on behalf of the Argentinean government. You know a country is REALLY screwed up when it has a dual exchange rate!

Dutch Disease — An economic condition that, in its broadest sense, refers to negative consequences arising from large increases to a country's income. Dutch disease is primarily associated with a natural resource discovery, but it can result from any large increase in foreign currency, including foreign direct investment, foreign aid or a substantial increase in natural resource prices. This condition arises when foreign currency inflows cause an increase in the affected country's currency. This has two main effects for the country with Dutch disease:

1. A decrease in the price competitiveness, and thus the exports, of its manufactured goods.

2. An increase in imports.

In the long run, both these factors can contribute to manufacturing jobs being moved to lower-cost countries. The end result is that non-resource industries are hurt by the increase in wealth generated by the resource-based industries. The term "*Dutch disease*" originates from a crisis in the Netherlands in the 1960s that resulted from discoveries of vast natural gas deposits in the North Sea. The newfound wealth caused the Dutch gilder to rise, making exports of all non-oil products less competitive on the world market. In the 1970s, the same economic condition occurred in Great Britain, when the price of oil quadrupled and it became economically viable to drill for North Sea Oil off the coast of Scotland. By the late 1970s, Britain had become a net exporter of oil; it had previously been a net importer. The pound soared in value, but the country fell into recession when British workers demanded higher wages and exports became uncompetitive. Critics say you can't blame such economic hardships on just one factor (say, rising oil prices) because there are so many other variables at play in the economy.

Economic Exposure — An exposure to fluctuating exchange rates, which affects a company's earnings, cash flow and foreign investments. The extent to which a company is affected by economic exposure depends on the specific characteristics of the company and its industry. Most large companies attempt to minimize the risk of fluctuating exchange rates by hedging with positions in the forex market.

Companies that do a lot of business in many countries, such as import/export companies, are at particular risk for economic exposure.

Equity Linked Foreign Exchange Option - ELF-X — A put or call option that protects an investor from foreign-exchange risk for a future sale or purchase of a specified foreign-equity portfolio. ELF-X options are a combination of a currency option and an equity forward contract. Should the exchange rate work in the investor's favor under the option contract, the total payout from the option is dependent upon the performance of the equities underlying the contract. Otherwise, the investor does not receive a payout. For example, if an investor holds an ELF-X call option on USD relative to CAD, and the Canadian dollar depreciates relative to the American, the investor would not receive a payout. However, if USD depreciated relative to CAD, the investor would receive the amount saved from use of the spot exchange rate in the option contract and the foreign-equity portfolio value, less the premium paid for the call option. Also known as a "*portfolio currency protection option*" or PCPO.

Euro LIBOR — London Interbank Offer Rate denominated in euros. This is the interest rate that banks offer each other for large short-term loans in euros. The rate is fixed once a day by a small group of large London banks but fluctuates throughout the day. This market makes it easier for banks to maintain liquidity requirements because they are able to quickly borrow from other banks that have surpluses. The Euro LIBOR is based on the average lending rates of 16 banks. These bank rates are available to the public through the British Bankers' Association. Euro LIBOR exists mainly for continuity purposes in swap contracts dating back to pre-euro times and is not very commonly used.

Eurocurrency Market — The money market in which Eurocurrency, currency held in banks outside of the country where it is legal tender, is borrowed and lent by banks in Europe. The Eurocurrency market allows for more convenient borrowing, which improves the international flow of capital for trade between countries and companies.

For example, a Japanese company borrowing U.S. dollars from a bank in France is using the Eurocurrency market.

European Central Bank – ECB —The central bank responsible for the monetary system of the European Union (EU) and the euro currency. The bank was formed in Germany in June 1998 and works with the other national banks of each of the EU members to formulate monetary policy that helps maintain price stability in the European Union. The European Central Bank has been responsible for the monetary policy of the European Union since January 1, 1999, when the euro currency was adopted by the EU members. The responsibilities of the ECB are to formulate monetary policy, conduct foreign exchange, hold currency reserves and authorize the issuance of bank notes, among many other things.

European Currency Quotation — An indirect quotation in the foreign exchange markets whereby the value of a foreign currency is stated as a per-unit measure of the U.S. dollar. This type of quotation shows how much foreign currency it takes to purchase one U.S. dollar. For example, a European currency quote would be C$1.24 per US$1. This explains that it will take 1.24 Canadian dollars to purchase a single unit of U.S. currency. If you wanted to purchase US$1,000 it would cost C$1,240.

European Monetary System – EMS — A 1979 arrangement between several European countries which links their currencies in an attempt to stabilize the exchange rate. This system was succeeded by the European Monetary Union (EMU), an institution of the European Union (EU), which established a common currency called the euro. The European Monetary System originated in an attempt to stabilize inflation and stop large exchange-rate fluctuations between European countries. Then, in June 1998, the European Central Bank was established and, in January 1999, a unified currency, the euro, was born and came to be used by most EU member countries.

European Economic and Monetary Union – EMU — The successor to the European Monetary System (EMS), the combination of European Union member states into a cohesive economic system, most notably represented with the adoption of the euro as the national currency of participating members. The EMU's succession over the EMS occurred through a three phase process, with the third and final phase initiating the adoption of the euro currency in place of former national currencies. This has been completed by all initial EU members except for the United Kingdom and Denmark, who have opted out of adopting the euro.

European Union – EU — A group of European countries that participates in the world economy as one economic unit and operates under one official currency, the euro. The EU's goal is to create a barrier-free trade zone and to enhance economic wealth by creating more efficiency within its marketplace. The current formalized incarnation of the European Union was created in 1993 with 12 initial members. Since then, many additional countries have since joined. The EU has become one of the largest producers in the world, in terms of GDP, and the euro has maintained a competitive value against the U.S. dollar. EU and non-EU members must agree to many legal requirements in order to trade with the EU member states.

Euroyen — Japanese yen-denominated deposits held in banks outside Japan. Also a term that refers to yen traded in the Eurocurrency market. An example of Euroyen would be yen deposits held in U.S. banks.

Eurozone — A geographic and economic region that consists of all the European Union countries that have fully incorporated the euro as their national currency. Also referred to as "*euroland*". The eurozone is one of the largest economic regions in the world and its currency, the euro, is considered one of the most liquid when compared to others. This region's currency continues to develop over time and is taking a more prominent position in the reserves of many central banks.

Exchange Control — Types of controls that governments put in place to ban or restrict the amount of foreign currency or local currency that is allowed to be traded or purchased. Common exchange controls include banning the use of foreign currency and restricting the amount of domestic currency that can be exchanged within the country. Typically, countries that employ exchange controls are those with weaker economies. These controls allow countries a greater degree of economic stability by limiting the amount of exchange rate volatility due to currency inflows/outflows. The International Monetary Fund has a provision called article 14, which only allows countries with transitional economies to employ foreign exchange controls.

Exchange Rate — An exchange rate is the rate at which one currency can be exchanged for another. In other words, it is the value of another country's currency compared to that of your own. If you are traveling to another country, you need to "*buy*" the local currency. Just like the price of any asset, the exchange rate is the price at which you can buy that currency. If you are traveling to Egypt, for example, and the exchange rate for U.S. dollars 1:5.5 Egyptian pounds, this means that for every U.S. dollar, you can buy five and a half Egyptian pounds. Theoretically, identical assets should sell at the same price in different countries, because the exchange rate must maintain the inherent value of one currency against the other. Did you know that the foreign exchange market (also known as FX or forex) is the largest market in the world? In fact, more than $3 trillion is traded in the currency markets on a daily basis as of 2009. *Fixed Exchange Rates*, There are two ways the price of a currency can be determined against another. A fixed, or pegged, rate is a rate the government (central bank) sets and maintains as the official exchange rate. A set price will be determined against a major world currency (usually the U.S. dollar, but also other major currencies such as the euro, the yen or a basket of currencies). In order to maintain the local exchange rate, the central bank buys and sells its own currency on the foreign exchange market in return for the currency to which it is pegged. If, for example, it is determined that the value of a single unit of local currency is equal to US$3, the central bank will have to ensure that it can supply the market with those dollars. In order to maintain the rate, the central bank must keep a high level of foreign reserves. This is a reserved amount of foreign currency held by the central bank that it can use to release (or absorb) extra funds into (or out of) the market. This ensures an appropriate money supply, appropriate fluctuations in the market (inflation/deflation), and ultimately, the exchange rate. The central bank can also adjust the official exchange rate when necessary. *Floating Exchange Rates*, unlike the fixed rate, a floating exchange rate is determined by the private market through supply and demand. A floating rate is often termed "self-correcting", as any differences in supply and demand will automatically be corrected in the market. Take a look at this simplified model: if demand for a currency is low, its value will decrease, thus making imported goods more expensive and stimulating demand for local goods and services. This in turn will generate more jobs, causing an auto-correction in the market. A floating exchange rate is constantly changing. In reality, no currency is wholly fixed or floating. In a fixed regime, market pressures can also influence changes in the exchange rate. Sometimes, when a local currency does reflect its true value against its pegged currency, a "*black market*", which is more reflective of actual supply and demand, may develop such as happened with the Brazilian Cruzado (before it was reissued as the Real by President Cardosa). A central bank will often then be forced to revalue or devalue the official rate so that the rate is in line with the unofficial one, thereby halting the activity of the black market. In a floating regime, the central bank may also intervene when it is necessary to ensure stability and to avoid inflation; however, it is less often that the central bank of a floating regime will interfere. The World Once Pegged, Between 1870 and 1914, there was a global fixed exchange rate. Currencies were linked to gold, meaning that the value of a local currency was fixed at a set exchange rate to gold ounces. This was known as the gold standard. This allowed for unrestricted capital mobility as well as global stability in currencies and trade; however, with the start of World War I, the gold standard was abandoned. At the end of World War II, the conference at Bretton Woods, an effort to generate global economic stability and increase global trade, established the basic rules and regulations governing international exchange. As such, an international monetary system, embodied in the International Monetary Fund (IMF), was established to promote foreign trade and to maintain the monetary stability of countries and therefore that of the global economy. (For further reading on the IMF, see What Is The International Monetary Fund?) It was agreed that currencies would once again be fixed, or pegged, but this time to the U.S. dollar, which in turn was pegged to gold at US$35 per ounce. What this meant was that the value of a currency was directly linked with the value of the U.S. dollar. So, if you needed to buy Japanese yen, the value of the yen would be expressed in U.S. dollars, whose value in turn was determined in the value of gold. If a country needed to readjust the value of its currency, it could approach the IMF to adjust the pegged value of its currency. The peg was maintained until 1971, when the U.S. dollar could no longer hold the value of the pegged rate of US$35 per ounce of gold. From then on, major governments adopted a floating system, and all attempts to move back to a global peg were eventually abandoned in 1985. Since then, no major economies have gone back to a peg, and the use of gold as a peg has been completely abandoned. Why Peg? The reasons to peg a currency are linked to stability. Especially in today's developing nations, a country may decide to peg its currency to create a stable atmosphere for foreign investment. With a peg, the investor will always know what his or her investment's value is, and therefore will not have to worry about daily fluctuations. A pegged currency can also help to lower inflation rates and generate demand, which results from greater confidence in the stability of the currency. Fixed regimes, however, can often lead to severe financial crises since a peg is difficult to maintain in the long run. This was seen in the Mexican (1995), Asian (1997) and Russian (1997) financial crises: an attempt to maintain a high value of the local currency to the peg resulted in the currencies eventually becoming overvalued. This meant that the governments could no longer meet the demands to convert the local currency into the foreign currency at the pegged rate. With speculation and panic, investors scrambled to get their money out and convert it into foreign currency before the local currency was devalued against the peg; foreign reserve supplies eventually became depleted. In Mexico's case, the government was forced to devalue the peso by 30%. In Thailand, the government eventually had to allow the currency to float, and by the end of 1997, the Thai bhat had lost 50% of its as the market's demand and supply readjusted the value of the local currency. Countries with pegs are often associated with having unsophisticated capital markets and weak regulating institutions. The peg is therefore there to help create stability in such an environment. It takes a stronger system as well as a mature market to maintain a float. When a country is forced to devalue its currency, it is also required to proceed with some form of economic reform, like implementing greater transparency, in an effort to strengthen its financial institutions. Some governments may choose to have a "floating," or "crawling" peg, whereby the government reassesses the value of the peg periodically and then changes the peg rate accordingly. Usually this causes devaluation, but it is controlled to avoid market panic. This method is often used in the transition from a peg to a floating regime, and it allows the government to "save face" by not being forced to devalue in an uncontrollable crisis. Although the peg has worked in creating global trade and monetary stability, it was used only at a time when all the major economies were a part of it. And while a floating regime is not without its flaws, it has proved to be a more efficient means of determining the long-term value of a currency and creating equilibrium in the international market.

Exchange Stabilization Fund – ESF — Money available to the U.S. Treasury Department primarily used for participating in the foreign-exchange market in an attempt to maintain currency stability. It holds U.S. dollars, foreign currencies and special drawing rights. The ESF allows the U.S. government to intervene in the forex market to influence exchange rates, usually the domain of the central bank, without affecting the domestic money supply. This money is also used to provide financing to foreign countries.

Finmins — Nickname given to the finance ministers from various countries who meet at global trade summits. Finance ministers are appointed and, depending on the country, the position can be given to an elected representative or to a non-elected official. The role played by a finance minister and the power he or she holds will vary among countries, but "*finmins*" are generally responsible for shaping or advising on the budget of a country and helping with other economic policies. This term is most often seen in the financial press, in reference to meetings between the financial ministers of various countries, especially the eurozone meetings. For example, you might see the headline, "*G7 finmins meet in Canada to discuss debt repayments from third world*".

Floating Exchange Rate — A country's exchange rate regime where its currency is set by the foreign-exchange market through supply and demand for that particular currency relative to other currencies. Thus, floating exchange rates change freely and are determined by trading in the forex market. This is in contrast to a "*fixed exchange rate*" regime. In some instances, if a currency value moves in any one direction at a rapid and sustained rate, central banks intervene by buying and selling its own currency reserves (i.e. Federal Reserve in the U.S.) in the foreign-exchange market in order to stabilize the local currency. However, central banks are reluctant to intervene, unless absolutely necessary, in a floating regime.

Foreign Currency Effects — The gain or loss on foreign investments due to changes in the relative value of assets denominated in a currency other than the principal currency with which a company normally conducts business. A rising domestic currency means foreign investments will result in lower returns when converted back to the domestic currency. The opposite is true for a declining domestic currency. Foreign investments are complicated by currency fluctuation and conversion between countries. A high quality investment in another country may prove worthless because of a weak currency. Foreign-denominated debt used to purchase domestic assets has led to bankruptcy in several cases due to a fast decline in a domestic currency or a rapid rise in the currency of the foreign-denominated debt.

Foreign Official Dollar Reserves – FRODOR — A term coined by economist Ed Yardeni relating international liquidity to the effect of foreign central banks on U.S. monetary policy. It is measured as the sum of U.S. Treasury and U.S. agency securities held by foreign banks. FRODOR is an extremely procyclical economic indicator. As the growth of FRODOR rises, so do the prices of stocks, commodities and real estate, while the U.S. dollar declines. The opposite is seen when the growth of FRODOR decelerates.

Forex Futures — An exchange-traded contract to buy or sell a specified amount of a given currency at a predetermined price on a set date in the future. All forex futures are written with a specific termination date, at which point delivery of the currency must occur unless an offsetting trade is made on the initial position. Forex futures serve two primary purposes as financial instruments. First, they can be used by companies or sole proprietors to remove the exchange-rate risk inherent in cross-border transactions. Second, they can be used by investors to speculate and profit from currency exchange-rate fluctuations.

Gnomes of Zurich — A term used by British labor ministers during the 1964 Sterling Crisis to refer to Swiss banks. British labor ministers were convinced that the foreign exchange speculation activities of Swiss banks were causing the devaluation of the Sterling. Just like the gnomes of legends, who dwell underground counting their riches, Swiss bankers were known for their extremely secretive policies. It was actually George Soros in New York behind it all.

Gold Standard — A monetary system in which a country's government allows its currency unit to be freely converted into fixed amounts of gold and vice versa. The exchange rate under the gold standard monetary system is determined by the economic difference for an ounce of gold between two currencies. The gold standard was mainly used from 1875 to 1914 and also during the interwar years. The use of the gold standard would mark the first use of formalized exchange rates in history. However, the system was flawed because countries needed to hold large gold reserves in order to keep up with the volatile nature of supply and demand for currency.   After World War II, a modified version of the gold standard monetary system, the Bretton Woods monetary system, was created as its successor. This successor system was initially successful, but because it also depended heavily on gold reserves, it was abandoned in 1971 when U.S President Nixon "*closed the gold window*".

Group of Eight - G-8 — Eight of the world's economically leading countries that in a cooperative effort meet periodically to address international economic and monetary issues. G-8 is considered global policy making at its highest level. The G-8 includes the Group of Seven countries along with Russia. Russia, although not a full member, has been in attendance since 1994.

Hard Currency — A currency, usually from a highly industrialized country, that is widely accepted around the world as a form of payment for goods and services. A hard currency is expected to remain relatively stable through a short period of time, and to be highly liquid in the Forex market. Another criterion for a hard currency is that the currency must come from a politically and economically stable country. The U.S. dollar and the British pound are good examples of hard currencies.

Indicative Quote — In forex trading, a currency quote that is provided by a market maker to a trading party but that is not firm. In other words, when a market maker provides an indicative quote to a trader, the market maker is not obligated to trade the given currency pair at the price or the quantity stated in the quote. Contrast this to a firm quote, in which a market maker guarantees a specified bid or ask price to a trader up to the maximum quantity specified in the quote. Market makers will typically provide indicative quotes if a trader requests a quote for a currency pair but does not specify the quantity to be traded, or if there is some doubt as to the market maker's ability to transact the currency pair at the bid or ask quoted. The bottom line is that traders can rely on indicative quotes as a reasonable estimate of the exchange rate at which they can enter their currency trade, but there is no guarantee that this will be the rate they get.

Indirect Quote — A foreign exchange rate quoted as the foreign currency per unit of the domestic currency. In an indirect quote, the foreign currency is a variable amount and the domestic currency is fixed at one unit. For example, in the U.S., an indirect quote for the Canadian dollar would be C$1.17 = US$1. Conversely, in Canada an indirect quote for U.S. dollars would be US$0.85 = C$1.

Interbank Market — The financial system and trading of currencies among banks and financial institutions, excluding retail investors and smaller trading parties. While some interbank trading is performed by banks on behalf of large customers, most interbank trading takes place from the banks' own accounts. The interbank market for forex serves commercial turnover of currency investments as well as a large amount of speculative, short-term currency trading. According to data compiled in 2004 by the Bank for International Settlements, approximately 50% of all Forex transactions are strictly interbank trades.

Interbank Rate — The rate of interest charged on short-term loans made between banks. Banks borrow and lend money in the interbank market in order to manage liquidity and meet the requirements placed on them. The interest rate charged depends on the availability of money in the market, on prevailing rates and on the specific terms of the contract, such as term length. Banks are required to hold an adequate amount of liquid assets, such as cash, to manage any potential withdrawals from clients. If a bank can't meet these liquidity requirements, it will need to borrow money in the interbank market to cover the shortfall. Some banks, on the other hand, have excess liquid assets above and beyond the liquidity requirements. These banks will lend money in the interbank market, receiving interest on the assets. There is a wide range of published interbank rates, including the LIBOR, which is set daily based on the average rates on loans made within the London interbank market.

Interest Rate Parity — A theory that the interest rate differential between two countries is equal to the differential between the forward exchange rate and the spot exchange rate. Interest rate parity plays an essential role in foreign exchange markets, connecting interest rates, spot exchange rates and foreign exchange rates.

The relationship can be seen when you follow the two methods an investor may take to convert foreign currency into U.S. dollars. Option A would be to invest the foreign currency locally at the foreign risk-free rate for a specific time period. The investor would then simultaneously enter into a forward rate agreement to convert the proceeds from the investment into U.S. dollars, using a forward exchange rate, at the end of the investing period. Option B would be to convert the foreign currency to U.S. dollars at the spot exchange rate, then invest the dollars for the same amount of time as in option A, at the local (U.S.) risk-free rate. When no arbitrage opportunities exist, the cash flows from both options are equal.

International Fisher Effect – IFE — An economic theory that states that an expected change in the current exchange rate between any two currencies is approximately equivalent to the difference between the two countries' nominal interest rates for that time. Calculated as:

$$E = \frac{i_1 - i_2}{1 + i_2} \approx i_1 - i_2$$

International Fisher Effect (IFE) Where:

"E" represents the % change in the exchange rate

"i1" represents country A's interest rate

"i2" represents country B's interest rate

For example, if country A's interest rate is 10% and country B's interest rate is 5%, country B's currency should appreciate roughly 5% compared to country A's currency. The rational for the IFE is that a country with a higher interest rate will also tend to have a higher inflation rate. This increased amount of inflation should cause the currency in the country with the high interest rate to depreciate against a country with lower interest rates.

International Monetary Fund – IMF — An international organization created for the purpose of:

1. Promoting global monetary and exchange stability.

2. Facilitating the expansion and balanced growth of international trade.

3. Assisting in the establishment of a multilateral system of payments for current transactions.

The IMF plays three major roles in the global monetary system. The Fund surveys and monitors economic and financial developments, lends funds to countries with balance-of-payment difficulties, and provides technical assistance and training for countries requesting it.

Inward Arbitrage — A form of arbitrage involving rearranging a bank's cash by borrowing from the interbank market, and re-depositing the borrowed money locally at a higher interest rate. The bank will make money on the spread between the interest rate on the local currency, and the interest rate on the borrowed currency. Inward arbitrage works because it allows the bank to borrow at a cheaper rate than it could in the local currency market. For example, assume an American bank goes to the Interbank market to borrow at the lower eurodollar rate, and then deposits those eurodollars at a bank within the US. The larger the spread, the more money that can be made.

Jennifer Lopez - J.Lo — A slang technical analysis term referring to a rounding bottom in a stock's price pattern. This term got its name from Jennifer Lopez's curvy figure; she is often criticized (or praised) for her round bottom. Traders like the rounding bottom in a stock pattern because it can be an indication of a positive market reversal, meaning expectations are gradually shifting from bearish to bullish. Ps. I HAD to throw this one in since I am a professor at the University of Puerto Rico and J.Lo is Puerto Rican!!!

London Interbank Mean Rate – LIMEAN — The mid-market rate in the London Interbank market, which is calculated by averaging the offer rate (LIBOR) and the bid rate (LIBID). The LIBOR is the rate at which funds are sold in the market, while the LIBID is the rate at which the funds are purchased in the market. The LIMEAN rate can be used by institutions borrowing and lending money in the interbank market, instead of using the LIBID or LIBOR rates, in any lending agreements. It can also be used to gain insight into the average rate at which money is being borrowed and lent in the interbank market.

Liquidation Level — In forex trading, the specific value of a trader's account below which the liquidation of the trader's positions is automatically triggered and executed at the best available exchange rate at the time. The liquidation level is expressed as a percentage value of assets. If a forex trader's positions go against him or her, his or her account will eventually reach the liquidation level, unless the trader contributes further margin to top up his or her account. Forex trading makes heavy use of leverage; therefore, the forex dealer holding an account for a trader takes on the risk that the trader's positions will lose money and that the trader will be unable to repay the borrowed funds used to make the forex trades. As such, a specified liquidation level, which the trader agrees to when opening his or her account, fixes the minimum margin (expressed as a percentage) that the forex dealer will tolerate before automatically liquidating the trader's assets to avoid the possibility of default.

Loonie — A slang term for a Canadian dollar. It is derived from the picture of a loon on one side of the coin. Just like in the U.S. where the dollar is referred to as the "*greenback*", the loonie is a often used to refer to the Canadian dollar. For example one may hear in a news report that the loonie was up in today's trade.

Monetary Base — The total amount of a currency that is either circulated in the hands of the public or in the commercial bank deposits held in the central bank's reserves. This measure of the money supply typically only includes the most liquid currencies. For example, suppose country Z has 600 million currency units circulating in the public and its central bank has 10 billion currency units in reserve as part of deposits from many commercial banks. In this case, the monetary base for country Z is 10.6 billion currency units. For many countries, the government can maintain a measure of control over the monetary base by buying and selling government bonds in the open market.

Moral Suasion — A persuasion tactic used by an authority (i.e. Federal Reserve Board) to influence and pressure, but not force, banks into adhering to policy. Tactics used are closed-door meetings with bank directors, increased severity of inspections, appeals to community spirit, or vague threats. A good example of moral suasion is when the Fed Chairman speaks on the markets - his opinion on the overall economy can send financial markets falling or flying. Often termed simply *"suasion"*, it has been used to persuade banks and other financial institutions to keep to official guidelines. The *"moral"* aspect comes from the pressure for *"moral responsibility"* to operate in a way that is consistent with furthering the good of the economy. In Australia, the Reserve Bank has show preference for this type of policy control. In Japan, it is known as *"window guidance"* and in the U.S., it is known as *"jawboning"* - exercising the persuasive power of talk rather than legislation.

Nominal Effective Exchange Rate – NEER — The unadjusted weighted average value of a country's currency relative to all major currencies being traded within an index or pool of currencies. The weights are determined by the importance a home country places on all other currencies traded within the pool, as measured by the balance of trade. The NEER represents the relative value of a home country's currency compared to the other major currencies being traded (U.S. dollar, Japanese yen, euro, etc.). A higher NEER coefficient (above 1) means that the home country's currency will usually be worth more than an imported currency, and a lower coefficient (below 1) means that the home currency will usually be worth less than the imported currency. The NEER also represents the approximate relative price a consumer will pay for an imported good.

Nonconvertible Currency — Any currency that is used primarily for domestic transactions and is not openly traded on a forex market. This usually is a result of government restrictions, which prevent it from being exchanged for foreign currencies. Also known as a "*blocked currency*". As the name implies, it is virtually impossible to convert a nonconvertible currency into other legal tender, except in limited amounts on the black market. When a nation's currency is nonconvertible it tends to limit the country's participation in international trade as well as distort its balance of trade.

Nostro Account — An account that a bank holds with a foreign bank. Nostro accounts are usually in the currency of the foreign country. This allows for easy cash management because currency doesn't need to be converted. Nostro is derived from the Latin term "*ours.*"

Outward Arbitrage — A form of arbitrage involving the rearrangement of a bank's cash by taking its local currency and depositing it into eurobanks. The interest rate will be higher in the interbank market, which will enable the bank to earn more on the interest it receives for the use of its cash. Outward arbitrage works because it allows the bank to lend for more abroad then it could in the local market. For example, assume an American bank goes to the interbank market to lend at the higher eurodollar rate. Money will be shifted from an American bank's branch within the U.S. to a branch located outside of the U.S. The bank will earn revenues on the spread between the two interest rates. The larger the spread, the more will be made.

Panel Bank — The name given to the group of banks contributing to the EURIBOR. This group is made up of the largest participants within the Euro money market. Panel bank institutions transact the largest volumes within the Euro market and provide stability and liquidity. Furthermore, these banks are located both inside and outside of Europe, and aren't always associated with regions recognizing the EU.

Parallel Loan — A type of foreign exchange loan agreement that was a precursor to currency swaps. A parallel loan involves two parent companies taking loans from their respective national financial institutions and then lending the resulting funds to the other company's subsidiary. For example, ABC, a Canadian company, would borrow Canadian dollars from a Canadian bank and XYZ, a French company, would borrow euros from a French bank. Then ABC would lend the Canadian funds to XYZ's Canadian subsidiary and XYZ would lend the euros to ABC's French subsidiary. The first parallel loans were implemented in the 1970s in the United Kingdom in order to bypass taxes that were imposed to make foreign investments more expensive.

Pegging — 1. A method of stabilizing a country's currency by fixing its exchange rate to that of another country. Most countries peg their exchange rate to that of the United States. 2. An investor writing a put option would practice pegging so that he or she will not be required, due to lowering prices, to purchase the underlying security or commodity from the option holder. The goal is to have the option expire worthless so that the premium initially received by the writer is protected. A practice of and investor buying large amounts of an underlying commodity or security close to the expiry date of a derivative held by the investor. This is done to encourage a favorable move in market price.

Purchasing Power Parity – PPP — An economic theory that estimates the amount of adjustment needed on the exchange rate between countries in order for the exchange to be equivalent to each currency's purchasing power. The relative version of PPP is calculated as:

$$S = \frac{P_1}{P_2}$$

Purchasing Power Parity (PPP)

Where:

"S" represents exchange rate of currency 1 to currency 2

"P1" represents the cost of good "x" in currency 1

"P2" represents the cost of good "x" in currency 2

In other words, the exchange rate adjusts so that an identical good in two different countries has the same price when expressed in the same currency.

For example, a chocolate bar that sells for C$1.50 in a Canadian city should cost US$1.00 in a U.S. city when the exchange rate between Canada and the U.S. is 1.50 USD/CDN. (Both chocolate bars cost US$1.00.)

Quote Currency —The second currency quoted in a currency pair in forex. In a direct quote, the quote currency is the foreign currency. In an indirect quote, the quote currency is the domestic currency. Also known as the "secondary currency" or "counter currency". Understanding the quotation and pricing structure of currencies is essential for anyone wanting to trade currencies in the forex market. If you were looking at the CAD/USD currency pair, the U.S. dollar would be the quote currency, and the Canadian dollar would be the base currency. Major currencies that are usually shown as the quote currency include the U.S. dollar, the British pound, the euro, the Japanese yen, the Swiss franc and the Canadian dollar.

Real Effective Exchange Rate – REER — The weighted average of a country's currency relative to an index or basket of other major currencies adjusted for the effects of inflation. The weights are determined by comparing the relative trade balances, in terms of one country's currency, with each other country within the index. This exchange rate is used to determine an individual country's currency value relative to the other major currencies in the index, as adjusted for the effects of inflation. All currencies within the said index are the major currencies being traded today: U.S. dollar, Japanese yen, euro, etc. This is also the value that an individual consumer will pay for an imported good at the consumer level. This price will include any tariffs and transactions costs associated with importing the good.

Redenomination — 1. The process whereby a country's currency is recalibrated due to significant inflation and currency devaluation. Certain currencies have been redenominated a number of times over the last century for various reasons. For example, the Bulgarian lev was redenominated due to inflation arising at the end of the Second World War. After the redenomination, one "new" lev was equal to 100 "old" levs. The lev was redenominated three times in the twentieth century. 2. The process of changing the currency value on a financial security. A recent example of redenomination arose when the euro was introduced and the denomination on many European securities had to be changed to the euro.

Repatriation — The process of converting a foreign currency into the currency of one's own country. The amount that the investor will receive depends on the exchange rate between the two currencies being traded at the settlement time. For example, if you are American, converting British pounds back to U.S. dollars is an example of repatriation. If the pound were held by a British financial institution, the dollars would be called eurodollars, therefore, when converting those eurodollars back to dollars, the investor would be exposed to foreign exchange risk.

Reserve Currency — A foreign currency held by central banks and other major financial institutions as a means to pay off international debt obligations, or to influence their domestic exchange rate. Currently, the U.S. dollar is the primary reserve currency used by other countries. A very large percentage of commodities such as gold and oil are usually priced in U.S dollars, causing other countries to hold this currency to pay for these goods. A large debate still continues about whether or not the U.S. dollar will stay the main reserve currency or if it will shift over to the euro.

Revaluation Rates — Market currency rates from a specific point in time that are used as a base value by currency traders to assess whether a profit or a loss has been realized for the day. In most cases, the revaluation rate is the closing rate for the previous trading day. For example, in order to assess how much profit a currency trader made today, he or she would use yesterday's closing rate (today's revaluation rate) of 1.15 USD/CAD as a baseline for comparing today's closing rate of 1.145 USD/CAD. If the trader shorts the U.S. dollar in early trading and then buys it back at the end of the day, he or she will make $0.005 for every U.S. dollar traded.

Seigniorage — The difference between the value of money and the cost to produce it - in other words, the economic cost of producing a currency within a given economy or country. If the seigniorage is positive, then the government will make an economic profit; a negative seigniorage will result in an economic loss. Seigniorage may be counted as revenue for a government when the money that is created is worth more than it costs to produce it. This revenue is often used by governments to finance a portion of their expenditures without having to collect taxes. If, for example, it costs the U.S. government $0.05 to produce a $1 bill, the seigniorage is $0.95, or the difference between the two amounts.

Soft Currency — Another name for "*weak currency*". The values of soft currencies fluctuate often, and other countries do not want to hold these currencies due to political or economic uncertainty within the country with the soft currency. Currencies from most developing countries are considered to be soft currencies. Often, governments from these developing countries will set unrealistically high exchange rates, pegging their currency to a currency such as the U.S. dollar.

Sovereign Risk — The risk that a foreign central bank will alter its foreign-exchange regulations thereby significantly reducing or completely nullifying the value of foreign-exchange contracts. This is one of the many risks that an investor faces when holding Forex contracts. Additionally an investor is exposed to interest-rate risk, price risk and liquidity risk amongst others.

Special Drawing Rights – SDR — An international type of monetary reserve currency, created by the International Monetary Fund (IMF) in 1969, which operates as a supplement to the existing reserves of member countries. Created in response to concerns about the limitations of gold and dollars as the sole means of settling international accounts, SDRs are designed to augment international liquidity by supplementing the standard reserve currencies. You can think of SDRs as an artificial currency used by the IMF and defined as a "basket of national currencies". The IMF uses SDRs for internal accounting purposes. SDRs are allocated by the IMF to its member countries and are backed by the full faith and credit of the member countries' governments.

Spot Exchange Rate — The rate of a foreign-exchange contract for immediate delivery. Also known as "*benchmark rates*", "*straightforward rates*" or "*outright rates*", spot rates represent the price that a buyer expects to pay for a foreign currency in another currency. Though the spot exchange rate is said to be settled immediately, the globally accepted settlement cycle for foreign-exchange contracts is two days. Foreign-exchange contracts are therefore settled on the second day after the day the deal is made.

Spot Trade — The purchase or sale of a foreign currency or commodity for immediate delivery. Spot trades are settled "on the spot", as opposed to at a set date in the future. Futures transactions that expire in the current month are also considered spot trades. Also known as "*cash trades*". Spot trades are the opposite of futures contracts, which usually expire well before any physical delivery. Foreign-exchange contracts are the most common kinds of spot trades. If these kinds of contracts are not settled immediately, traders would expect to be compensated for the time value of their money for the duration of the delivery. Since these contracts are settled electronically, the Forex market is essentially instantaneous.

Sterilization — A form of monetary action in which a central bank or federal reserve attempts to insulate itself from the foreign exchange market to counteract the effects of a changing monetary base. The sterilization process is used to manipulate the value of one domestic currency relative to another, and is initiated in the forex market. For example, to weaken the U.S. dollar against another currency, the Fed would sell more U.S. dollars and buy the foreign currency. The increased supply of the U.S. dollar would lower the value of the currency. The Fed would do the opposite if it wanted to strengthen the U.S. dollar.

Sterilized Intervention — A method used by monetary authorities to equalize the effects of foreign exchange transactions on the domestic monetary base by offsetting the purchase or sale of domestic assets within the domestic markets. The process limits the amount of domestic currency available for foreign exchange. Sterilized intervention is a way for a country to alter its debt composition without affecting its monetary base. It is used to counter undesirable exchange-rate movements. For example, a decrease in the value of a country's domestic currency would cause a debt instrument issued in a foreign country and denominated in that foreign country's currency to be made more expensive.

Swissie — A slang term for the Swiss franc. The Swiss franc, or Swissie, has often been considered a safe-haven currency during times of geopolitical unrest. This is mainly due to the country's neutral stance in global conflicts. For example, one may hear in a news report that the Swissie was down in today's trading. This is similar to the U.S., where the dollar is referred to as the "greenback", Canada, where the dollar is called a "loonie" and New Zealand, where the dollar is called a "kiwi".

Temporal Method — A method of foreign currency translation that uses exchange rates based on the time assets and liabilities are acquired or incurred. The exchange rate used also depends on the method of valuation that is used. Assets and liabilities valued at current costs use the current exchange rate and those that use historical exchange rates are valued at historical costs. By using the temporal method, any income-generating assets like inventory, property, plant and equipment are regularly updated to reflect their market values. The gains and losses that result from translation are placed directly into the current consolidated income. This causes the consolidate earnings to be rather volatile.

Transaction Exposure — The risk, faced by companies involved in international trade, that currency exchange rates will change after the companies have already entered into financial obligations. Such exposure to fluctuating exchange rates can lead to major losses for firms. Often, when a company identifies such exposure to changing exchange rates, it will choose to implement a hedging strategy, using forward rates to lock in an exchange rate and thus eliminate the exposure to the risk.

Transaction Risk — The exchange rate risk associated with the time delay between entering into a contract and settling it. The greater the time differential between the entrance and settlement of the contract, the greater the transaction risk, because there is more time for the two exchange rates to fluctuate. Transaction risk creates difficulties for individuals and corporations dealing in different currencies, as exchange rates can fluctuate significantly over a short period of time. This volatility is usually reduced, or hedged, by entering into currency swaps and other similar securities.

Translation Exposure — The risk that a company's equities, assets, liabilities or income will change in value as a result of exchange rate changes. This occurs when a firm denominates a portion of its equities, assets, liabilities or income in a foreign currency. Also known as "*accounting exposure*". Accountants use various methods to insulate firms from these types of risks, such as consolidation techniques for the firm's financial statements and the use of the most effective cost accounting evaluation procedures. In many cases, this exposure will be recorded in the financial statements as an exchange rate gain (or loss).

Translation Risk — The exchange rate risk associated with companies that deal in foreign currencies or list foreign assets on their balance sheets. The greater the proportion of asset, liability and equity classes denominated in a foreign currency, the greater the translation risk. This poses a serious threat for companies conducting business in foreign markets. Exchange rates usually change between quarterly financial statements, causing significant variances between the reported figures. Companies attempt to minimize these transaction risks by purchasing currency swaps or hedging through futures contracts.

Uncovered Interest Rate Parity – UIP — A parity condition stating that the difference in interest rates between two countries is equal to the expected change in exchange rates between the countries' currencies. If this parity does not exist, there is an opportunity to make a profit.

$$(i_1 - i_2) = E(e)$$

Uncovered Interest Rate Parity (UIP) where…

"i1" represents the interest rate of country 1

"i2" represents the interest rate of country 2

"E(e)" represents the expected rate of change in the exchange rate

For example, assume that the interest rate in America is 10% and the interest rate in Canada is 15%. According to the uncovered interest rate parity, the Canadian dollar is expected to depreciate against the American dollar by approximately 5%. Put another way, to convince an investor to invest in Canada when its currency depreciates, the Canadian dollar interest rate would have to be about 5% higher than the American dollar interest rate.

Unsterilized Foreign Exchange Intervention — An attempt by a country's monetary authorities to influence exchange rates and its money supply by not buying or selling domestic or foreign currencies or assets. This is a passive approach to exchange rate fluctuations, and allows for fluctuations in the monetary base. If the central bank purchases domestic currency by selling foreign assets, the money supply will shrink because it has removed domestic currency from the market; this is an example of a sterilized policy. An unsterilized policy allows for the foreign-exchange markets to function without manipulation of the supply of the domestic currency; therefore, the monetary base is allowed to change.

U.S. Dollar Index – USDX — A measure of the value of the U.S. dollar relative to majority of its most significant trading partners. This index is similar to other trade-weighted indexes, which also use the exchange rates from the same major currencies. Currently, this index is calculated by factoring in the exchange rates of six major world currencies: the euro, Japanese yen, Canadian dollar, British pound, Swedish krona and Swiss franc. This index started in 1973 with a base of 100 and is relative to this base. This means that a value of 120 would suggest that the U.S. dollar experienced a 20% increase in value over the time period. It is possible to incorporate futures or options strategies on the USDX. These financial products currently trade on the New York Board Of Trade.

Xenocurrency — A currency that trades in markets outside of its domestic borders. "Xeno" is a prefix meaning foreign or strange. An example of a xenocurrency is the Chinese yuan when it is traded in the United States. When currency is deposited by national governments or corporations in banks outside their home market, it is sometimes referred to as a "*eurocurrency*" (this applies to any currency and to banks in any country).

DISCLAIMER

THE DATA CONTAINED HEREIN IS BELIEVED TO BE RELIABLE BUT CANNOT BE GUARANTEED AS TO RELIABILITY, ACCURACY, OR COMPLETENESS; AND, AS SUCH ARE SUBJECT TO CHANGE WITHOUT NOTICE. WE WILL NOT BE RESPONSIBLE FOR ANYTHING, WHICH MAY RESULT FROM RELIANCE ON THIS DATA OR THE OPINIONS EXPRESSED HEREIN.

DISCLOSURE OF RISK:

THE RISK OF LOSS IN TRADING FUTURES, FOREX AND OPTIONS CAN BE SUBSTANTIAL; THEREFORE, ONLY GENUINE RISK FUNDS SHOULD BE USED. FUTURES, FOREX AND OPTIONS MAY NOT BE SUITABLE INVESTMENTS FOR ALL INDIVIDUALS, AND INDIVIDUALS SHOULD CAREFULLY CONSIDER THEIR FINANCIAL CONDITION IN DECIDING WHETHER TO TRADE. OPTION TRADERS SHOULD BE AWARE THAT THE EXERCISE OF A LONG OPTION WOULD RESULT IN A FUTURES OR FOREX POSITION.

HYPOTHETICAL PERFORMANCE RESULTS HAVE MANY INHERENT LIMITATIONS, SOME OF WHICH ARE DESCRIBED BELOW.

NO REPRESENTATION IS BEING MADE THAT ANY ACCOUNT WILL, OR IS LIKELY TO, ACHIEVE PROFITS OR LOSSES SIMILAR TO THOSE SHOWN. IN FACT, THERE ARE FREQUENTLY SHARP DIFFERENCES BETWEEN HYPOTHETICAL PERFORMANCE RESULTS AND THE ACTUAL RESULTS SUBSEQUENTLY ACHIEVED BY ANY PARTICULAR TRADING PROGRAM.

ONE OF THE LIMITATIONS OF HYPOTHETICAL PERFORMANCE RESULTS IS THAT THEY ARE GENERALLY PREPARED WITH THE BENEFIT OF HINDSIGHT. IN ADDITION, HYPOTHETICAL TRADING DOES NOT INVOLVE FINANCIAL RISK, AND NO HYPOTHETICAL TRADING RECORD CAN COMPLETELY ACCOUNT FOR THE IMPACT OF FINANCIAL RISK IN ACTUAL TRADING. FOR EXAMPLE, THE ABILITY TO WITHSTAND LOSSES OR TO ADHERE TO A PARTICULAR TRADING PROGRAM, IN SPITE OF TRADING LOSSES, THERE ARE MATERIAL POINTS WHICH CAN ALSO ADVERSELY AFFECT ACTUAL TRADING RESULTS. THERE ARE NUMEROUS OTHER FACTORS RELATED TO THE MARKETS, IN GENERAL, OR TO THE IMPLEMENTATION OF ANY SPECIFIC TRADING PROGRAM WHICH CANNOT BE FULLY ACCOUNTED FOR IN THE PREPARATION OF HYPOTHETICAL PERFORMANCE RESULTS AND ALL OF WHICH CAN ADVERSELY AFFECT ACTUAL TRADING RESULTS.

High Risk Investment

Off-exchange foreign currency trading on margin, Futures on Margin, Options, or Stock Trading all carry a high level of risk and may not be suitable for all investors. The high degree of leverage can work against you as well as for you. Before deciding to invest you should carefully consider your investment objectives, level of experience, and risk appetite. The possibility exists that you could sustain a loss of some or all of your initial investment and, therefore, you should not invest money that you cannot afford to lose. You should be aware of all the risks associated with off-exchange foreign currency trading and seek advice from an independent financial advisor if you have any doubts.

Testimonial Disclaimer

Unique experiences and past performances do not guarantee future results! Testimonials herein are unsolicited and are non-representative of all clients. The Right To Wealth or Gecko Software opinions, news, research, analyses, prices, or other information contained on this website is provided as general market commentary, and does not constitute investment advice. Doc Brown & The Delano Max Wealth Institute will not accept liability for any loss or damage, including without limitation to, any loss of profit, which may arise directly or indirectly from use of or reliance on such information, products or services.

Trading Risks

There are risks associated Futures, Forex, and options as well as utilizing an Internet-based deal execution trading system including, but not limited to, the failure of hardware, software, and Internet connection. Since The Right To Wealth or Gecko Software do not control your trading decisions, signal power, its reception or routing via Internet, configuration of your equipment or reliability of its connection, we cannot be responsible for communication failures, distortions or delays when trading via the Internet.

Accuracy of Information

The content on this website and in The Right To Wealth or Gecko Software is subject to change at any time without notice, and is provided for the sole purpose of assisting traders to make independent investment decisions. Doc Brown & The Delano Max Wealth Institute have taken reasonable measures to ensure the accuracy of the information on the website, however, we do not guarantee its accuracy, and will not accept liability for any loss or damage which may arise directly or indirectly from the content or your inability to access the website, for any delay in or failure of the transmission or the receipt of any instruction or notifications sent through this website.

Distribution

This course is not intended for distribution, or use by, any person in any country where such distribution or use would be contrary to local law or regulation. None of the services or investments referred to in this website are available to persons residing in any country where the provision of such services or investments would be contrary to local law or regulation. It is the responsibility of visitors to this website to ascertain the terms of and comply with any local law or regulation to which they are subject.

Market Risks and Online Trading

The trading platform provides sophisticated order entry and tracking of orders. All stop-loss, limit and entry orders are guaranteed against slippage except in extraordinary volatile market conditions. Trading on-line, no matter how convenient or efficient does not necessarily reduce risks associated with currency trading. All quotes and trades are subject to the terms and conditions of the Client Agreement accessible through this website.

www.ingramcontent.com/pod-product-compliance
Lightning Source LLC
Chambersburg PA
CBHW081116170526
45165CB00008B/2463